LIFE
EXPERIENCE

leisure & culture DUBLIN

Nicola Simpson

Yellow Rose Publishing Ltd

First published in United Kingdom in 2012 by

Yellow Rose Publishing Ltd

A CIP catalogue record for this title is available from the British Library

ISBN 978-0-9574098-0-4

Printed and bound by Lightening Source UK Ltd

Disclaimer

I have tried to recreate events, locales and conversations from my memories of them. In order to maintain their anonymity in some instances I have changed the names of individuals and may have changed some identifying characteristics.

You will come across several swear words throughout this book. I felt if I removed them it wouldn't show the true reality of how I felt, so they have stayed.

I apologise if you find them offensive.

Dedicated to:

My Beautiful Daughters

Abigail & Hannah

Sisters by Heart

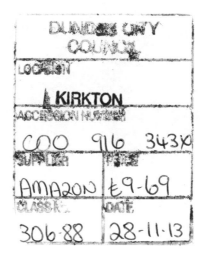

KIRKTON

Acknowledgments

To put down in words the tragic events of the end of my daughter's life and the pain that came with it, filled me with dread. I honestly thought I couldn't do it.

So, firstly my sincere gratitude and thanks to my friend Clare Muir who planted the seed within me to write Abigail's Rainbow. With her support and encouragement I felt I could do this for others, for people to understand some of what goes on behind closed doors, to understand that the pain and suffering they themselves may be going through is normal and also that when you smile and feel happy that it's alright to feel the pleasure of life once more.

Thank you to Paul, Abigail's father, who shares with me the grief and pain of living without her every day. We have been through so much together over the years, he has been my rock and I couldn't have got through this without him.

I owe our daughter Hannah so much; she has always given me the space and time to write. Often I have been sitting with her but I have not been present for my thoughts and attention has been here. She is a star and I love her with all my heart.

Paphos Writers Group in Cyprus have sat and listened to what I have written and seen for themselves, the pain I have been through. I have struggled to read some of these chapters, reliving my heartache. The Group's advice, feedback and support has been wonderful. A special thank you to John Goodwin, author of "The Last Olympiad" who has supported and edited my book from beginning to end along the way. Cheers John, my surrogate dad.

Steve, who came with me to Bellapais in Northern Cyprus to help with my first edit, was the first to read it all from cover to cover, the first to really see inside my head and my heart, a bit of a scary prospect really. His dedication to reading every day; he scrutinised, questioned and was most of all honest. Thank you.

To Kate Fensom, my wonderful friend who gave me permission to use her painting "The Peace Garden" for marketing and publicity. Also, to her magnificent husband Max Dane who kindly brought the front cover together for me and set up my website. I love it and I know Abigail would have too.

Thanks to my friend Clara Baxter who lent me her copy of the Writers' & Artists' Yearbook to help me find an agent and publisher. Her book has travelled with me everywhere, I have read and re-read and exhausted every avenue; it's been an amazing journey.

To my cousin Luke who has undoubtedly saved me; by making me re-think some of the wording and phrases I have used!

All of my new social networking friends on the internet, the tremendous support that has been shown to me has been absolutely amazing, you have all followed my story from newspaper features to radio and television interviews where I have been terrified and excited. Thank you all so much for being there for me.

And finally Robin, the last leg of my journey, thank you for agreeing to meet me for lunch, I know it was only meant to be an hour. But you allowed me to pick your brains for over three! Your experience in the literary field has been an enormous help, I really can't thank you enough for bridging the gap and teaching me the next steps. My book is finally published!

The list of names to thank is endless. I apologise to those who may feel that their name has been missed. I can assure you it hasn't, you know who you are and my sincere thanks goes out to you all.

I have received an enormous amount of support and guidance from friends, family and even strangers along the difficult journey of writing this book. To all of you I am eternally grateful: thank you.

Preface

For the number of words
Written here in this book
There's the same again
Still in my head

Too sore to bear
The emotions to share
From my head to my heart
The pain is still there

The Beginning is the End

So, where do I start? This has been my dilemma for such a long time; but the truth is that the beginning of my story is the tragic end of my beautiful daughter Abigail's life.

It's every parent's worst nightmare. Eleven twenty pm the door bell rang. Expecting it to be Abigail, I opened the door. Forgot her key, I thought.

I looked straight past the policeman standing on my doorstep, expecting to see Abigail behind him, anger whirling up inside me, dreading to hear what she'd done. Abigail pushed me to the limits at times: she could definitely be cheeky, but in a pleasant way always with a smile. A typical teenager. She didn't break the law though, so I wondered why he was here.

'Is Abigail with you?' I asked, looking round him.

'No,' he replied. His voice was calm, his face giving nothing away.

I asked him to come in, feeling puzzled. I kept asking where Abigail was. She was due home by now and I was worried.

Stood in my hallway he said,

'There's been a fatal accident. We think Abigail may have been involved. Can you tell me what she was wearing please?'

Shocked, an accident. I racked my brain to think.

'Erm, her jeans,' I couldn't remember what top she had on, my mind whizzing, everything a blur. 'Er, a green top I think and her cream sleeveless jacket. Can I go and see her?'

All I could see in my head was her lying in a hospital bed unconscious with tubes everywhere. Still having no idea what 'fatal' meant I asked again if I could go to the hospital to be with her. I asked if he could breathalyse me because I'd had a glass of wine that night and I didn't drink and drive, not even one drink, ever. But I needed to go and be with Abigail, this was an emergency. I felt sober and Ok to drive.

There seemed a long delay to all of my questions. Then he replied that he didn't have the kit with him because he was in an unmarked police car. I felt confused.

I heard Paul cry out in the kitchen. I went to him and held him tight. 'She'll be Ok,' I said, trying to reassure him.

We went into the living room where the policeman was now sitting on the sofa. In shock we asked more questions. 'Where was she? Who was she with? Where was the accident? Can we go there? Can we be with Abigail?' the list went on.

Paul looked confused and then asked the question, 'How serious is fatal?'

I turned and stared at the police officer, waiting for his answer.

That's when he said it.

'I'm sorry, she died.'

Time stopped.

We froze. Numb inside, unable to speak, unable to think.

I shook my head.

'Sorry, what did you say?' this couldn't be real, not Abigail, not our daughter. We just sat there, staring at the floor. Silent. I looked at Paul and saw the tears on his face. Our world had just ended.

* * *

Abigail had been due home at eleven that night. Abigail being Abigail was always about ten minutes late. Typical teenager trying to push the boundaries! At about ten thirty I'd had a sickening feeling that something was wrong. I didn't know why, but I felt sick to my stomach. I was sat on the floor in our living room re-covering the blind for our kitchen. At ten fifty I started to try and call her, no answer, just that awful lady's voice telling me it's not possible to connect my call or one of those kinds of messages. I heard it over and over again every time I picked up the phone and pressed redial. I continuously called her but always no answer. Paul started to worry and wanted to go out and look for her.

'No, it's Ok,' I told him, 'she'll be home soon.' Inside I was worried sick but also suspected I was just being paranoid.

I was worried that she was going to be mugged, attacked, raped, something horrible like that, but never this. I was scared and just wanted to speak to her.

We lived in Scrabster a couple of miles outside the town of Thurso. I just wanted to tell her to get a taxi home. I kept visualising her walking in the front door upset, holding her face with her hair all in a mess. I didn't once imagine she was never coming home.

* * *

As I write this I can hear a car in the distance with a very loud exhaust and it sounds like they're speeding. I assume a *He*, politically correct or not it is often young lads who cause these horrific accidents. Why is that?

Do they think they're indestructible? They drive without a care in the world. Not concerned at all for their passengers or other road-users. They will only learn the hard way, when another family has to grieve for their precious child. I wish I could make them all sit down and listen and realise the dangers, but I can't and I can't change the world on my own.

* * *

The last time I saw Abigail was in our kitchen. I had this horrible feeling inside, something wasn't right. I told her and her friend Meghan to both be good and not do anything silly. I told her I didn't want any phone calls that night. I remember Abigail's reply,

'Don't worry Mum we learnt our lesson last time.'

Abigail was referring to an incident six months earlier when they were staying at their friend Ellen's house in Castletown. They'd fallen out with Ellen and later that night Ellen had told them they couldn't stay. Far from home and worried they were going to be in trouble they'd decided to wait for a friend of Meghan's parents to come home and ask to stay at her house instead. In the meantime Ellen's father called me to tell me that Abigail hadn't arrived at his home. Of course like any parent, I went MAD, BALLISTIC in fact, and Abigail was grounded for a month. So of course, I put my feelings down to that night. The terrible twosome!

Abigail was taken from us when she was only fifteen, still a child. She left home with Meghan, to meet their friends and go to a party in Castletown on Saturday 6th October 2007. The worst day of my life. I hate this date, even to see it written makes my chest feel tight and takes my breath away.

Abigail was very attractive, stunning in fact; but then I'm biased because I'm her mum. It wasn't surprising that most of the boys seemed to fancy her. She was a bubbly, bright but also ditsy Essex girl (we are very proud to be Essex girls.) So, when the boys were having a party in Castletown and called to invite her, of course she accepted. Like any young girl, she was flattered by all the attention. Loved it, in fact. I understand she waited with her friends in Thurso for Scott to drive into town to collect them.

Scott pulled up outside Robins fish and chip shop in Thurso in his Ford Fiesta. Abigail and her friend got in the back of the car; Abigail sitting behind the front passenger on the nearside. Scott, eighteen years old, hadn't been drinking but had passed his test just three days earlier. They drove off and went to Scrabster Harbour. Probably showing off, I understand that the lad in the back then got in the boot of the car. They drove back into Thurso and picked up another girl Hazel who was waiting for them.

Then they set off for the party. I believe as they turned onto the Thurso to Castletown road Scott saw his friend's car in front of him. Young, inexperienced and foolish Scott and his friend overtook each other several times along the main road. As Scott drove into Castletown he ignored the thirty miles per hour sign and sped into the village. As he turned the corner he lost control, clipped the kerb and hit a pillar at the end of the wall. Abigail took the full impact.

There's no way she could have survived. She died there at the scene.

I later heard Tyrone, the driver of the other car, pulled over and called the police. His two female passengers ran to the scene and assisted those in the car. A very brave act for both of them, it must have been hugely difficult to deal with.

Myself, Paul, our daughter Hannah, family and friends have all been left devastated. It wasn't until weeks and months later that we realised just how much Abigail's passing affected our community. She touched so many people.

* * *

I remembered all the lovely things we'd done that day, all the little things we had giggled at. We moved into our new house only the week before and I was busy painting the kitchen and dining room.

I bought Abigail and Hannah hamsters as pets just a week earlier. Desperate to have a pet, I had promised them both they could have hamsters once we'd moved in. I kept my promise. They'd cleaned their hamster home earlier that morning. It wasn't a cage like most, more a multi-coloured plastic contraption that looked like something out of space. It all came apart and looked difficult to put back together but they managed. I could hear them in the utility room. It was so funny listening to their conversation about hamster poo.

Abigail came through to the kitchen, picked up the paint tin and read the name on the side 'Mmm cookie dough' she said. Thinking it sounded delicious she asked if she could taste it. I rolled my eyes and shook my head, typical Abigail. She laughed and said 'Only joking' then went on to paint the wall. If I'd said yes she probably would have licked the tin!

I told Paul what a lovely day we'd all had and how I hadn't moaned or shouted at her once. I'd been so stressed by the move that I think I lost my rag most days and Abigail seemed to bear the brunt of it. I wish she hadn't, I wish I'd been a better Mum. It had been a wonderful day, perfect in fact; full of laughter, smiles and giggles.

Paul had been working long hours for a few days and hadn't seen Abigail since the Thursday before. I know this eats away at him.

When I finally got the paint brush back Abigail asked what was for lunch. She looked in the freezer and found Peking-Duck. You should have seen her face. It broke into an enormous beaming smile. She was really excited, this was one of her favourite meals. She couldn't contain herself and made me laugh out loud, a real tummy tickler. She insisted we needed cucumber and spring onions of course.

Having none in the house she searched for a suitable handbag to go shopping with. It wasn't cool for Abigail to use a carrier bag, especially from the shop she normally went to and she would be so annoyed if I mentioned it here. Convinced she had the right bag she set off for the shop with Hannah. Half an hour later they returned, Hannah carrying the cucumber, handbag too small! They were laughing so much, absolutely roaring. It was wonderful to hear them. At last our family were back to normal and in our own home.

We had had a nightmare trying to move house for nearly two years. We lost several properties for one reason or another and it had been a really stressful time for all of us. We'd lived with my Mum in Spittal, a very rural village in Caithness, for the last four months and things had been very tense. We were all looking forward to having our own home again and our new house was perfect. We loved it, our dream home in a really desirable area. Having moved several times over the years this house was finally the 'Home,' we had been searching for for such a long time.

Abigail made the crispy duck pancakes for the three of us and they were delicious. Later, after the accident Hannah told me that they had been singing Christmas songs and Kumbaya My Lord, only they were singing Kumba bananas while walking to the shop and back.

Abigail, delighted with herself for making lunch, had offered to make dinner too so again we were having one of her favourites, chicken curry. I think Abigail probably had enough favourite meals to have one every day of the week.

She waved her hands around the kitchen and told me to make sure I had cleaned all the mess up before she got home.

'Only joking,' she laughed again, but I knew she meant it really.

The girls went out with their friends that afternoon. I finished painting and decided to go and buy material so that I could cover the blind and finish the room completely. I returned home, cleaned the kitchen and started to make dinner. Abigail was running late so I knew she wouldn't mind. Abigail came home with Meghan full of their afternoon and was happy for me to be cooking.

Hannah had asked if she could stay over at her friend's that night. The house seemed chaotic, filled with the noise and laughter of normal family life. Abigail and Meghan were talking about the new furniture I had ordered for our dining room. Abigail described the high backed brown leather chairs in great detail; it was so funny she even showed Meghan how you sat on them in mid air. She was as excited as I was about our new home. Abigail had helped me choose the colours for every room.

We spent months reading magazines and looking through brochures; designing and planning. We collected pictures from magazines while choosing the style of her bedroom; black and white, very sleek and elegant. We bought the house from our friend Maria, Abigail's first boyfriend Liam's mum.

We got the keys to our new home late on the afternoon of Monday 24th September 2007. Paul and I decorated both the girls' rooms and the spare bedroom within three days of taking possession. Fortunately we didn't have to strip any wallpaper. The walls were all painted so all we had to do was sand them down, repaint and wallpaper one feature wall in each of the girls' rooms. I had arranged for carpet to be fitted first thing Friday morning before the lorry arrived with all our belongings. I was confident we would be finished in time.

Abigail's room looked exactly as we had planned when her friends came to see it after school with her. They loved it too. 'Wow, I want a room like this' was the comment I heard most from her friends as they ran into her new bedroom. She helped choose bathroom tiles and furniture. I remember her asking me if I would decorate her house when she left home. It was all so exciting, new home, new furniture, everything seemed so perfect.   But when Abigail went out with her friends that night she never came home, our family was destroyed.

'I scream, but nobody can hear me'

The Next Painful Steps

Sitting with the police officer, staring into space, not knowing what to do or say; he asked where our family were. My Mum lives in Caithness but the rest of our family all live in Essex. He offered to drive us to my Mum's, I didn't want to. I didn't want to see anyone or be with anyone except Paul at that moment. I just wanted Abigail to come home. I couldn't believe she had died: surely not, not my baby. I had seen her only a few hours ago, laughing and joking, this just couldn't be real. It couldn't be my daughter; this wasn't happening to us, not really, but it was.

The policeman left us; he said we could contact him anytime through the night and he would come back for us if we needed him. The next few hours are a blur. I remember crying, sitting stunned, Paul and I just looking into space then at each other.

Do we go and get Hannah in the middle of the night to tell her? No. We decided to let her sleep and get her early the next morning from her friends. Our lives had all been turned upside down in one split second; life as we knew it no longer existed.

Paul and I kept asking each other what we should do. Should we call our family? Should we go to my Mum's? We didn't know. I didn't want to wake anyone up and tell them this unspeakable news; I couldn't believe it myself let alone tell anyone. I kept thinking what difference would it make telling them now or in the morning. I decided to let them all sleep; we couldn't be together, we lived too far apart.

But later, I finally decided that it was best to call my sister who was always up late at the weekend and slept in until Sunday afternoon. I wouldn't want to wake her in the morning so I called her first. I remember telling her I had some really bad news and telling her what had happened. I can still hear the pain in her voice as she cried out. Her partner Casey immediately took the phone. I repeated what happened and put the phone down. I was numb, my hands shaking, a total mess. I sat and cried with Paul, I sobbed. This was awful enough as it was, but now I had the horrendous job of gradually telling everyone else. But I had to do it. I didn't want any of our family to hear from someone else. It had to be me.

In the early hours of the morning we decided we should tell my Mum and Weyland, my stepdad. Paul called the police officer who had come to our home earlier to ask him if he would drive us to my mum's. He had offered to tell her for us but I knew it was best that I did and asked him to come in with us. I have no idea what time it was. My Mum and Weyland were both asleep. I knocked on their bedroom window to wake them. Weyland came and answered the door; it was obvious something was wrong. My face would have said it all, Paul by my side with the police officer behind us. I asked for my Mum. She had gone to the bathroom. I heard her call out that she wouldn't be a minute. Paul, Weyland, the police officer and I sat in the living room in silence looking at the floor and then at each other. Weyland looked concerned, he knew something was wrong but he had to sit there and wait. I wasn't going to say it twice. We waited; the seconds felt like an eternity. It was horrible.

This was the worst thing I have had to do in my entire life I thought. Telling my family that my daughter had been killed is not something you ever expect to have to do. But little did I know then that there were so many more awful days to deal with still to come.

When my mum joined us, I somehow managed to say it and I sat and hugged her for what felt like forever. Eventually we stopped and sat in silence, once again staring at the carpet. There was nothing to say and nothing we could do.

Looking back I can't believe that I was being asked in the middle of the night, just a few hours after being told my daughter had died, whether Abigail was to be buried or cremated and where her funeral would be. Choices I couldn't even contemplate and so I made quick decisions in a panic, trying to think but couldn't. I was also being told that I needed to go to Inverness over a hundred miles from my home to identify her body at nine am Monday morning. We had to go to the police headquarters there, yet we had no idea where this was. I know the police were doing their best to investigate what had happened that night but expecting us to drive such a long distance that early in the morning under the circumstances seemed ludicrous to me.

I suddenly said 'I wonder if Abigail wanted to be an organ donor?' None of us knew. I looked at the policeman who then told me that I would need to discuss this on Monday when we went to identify her. I couldn't stop thinking about it and finally decided that, yes, I would allow her to be a donor. Abigail could help so many others to have a better life, she would have wanted that.

When he dropped us off at home he asked if there was anything he could do, anyone he could call for us. The only thing I could think of was to tell the school. I had to do the rest.

Paul and I went home; we sat on the sofa cuddled up together, silent, in tears. Suddenly I panicked. I couldn't remember what Abigail looked like. I'd only seen her a few hours ago, how could I forget what my own daughter looked like? I was in shock. I went into our garden room to get the box of photos that we hadn't yet unpacked. Paul and I went through them all, a whole life of memories, of tears and smiles, special memories that we will treasure forever. Eventually we went to bed and just lay there sobbing, hugging each other; of course we didn't sleep. I remember wanting to sell the house and just move. I thought then that moving there was the worst thing we could have ever done.

The next morning we went to tell Hannah. How do you tell your daughter what has happened to her sister? It was horrendous. As a parent you want to protect your children from anything and everything. I couldn't protect my girls. I couldn't stop this horrible roller coaster that we were now on. So many dreadful things to do, this was worse than telling my Mum.

I started to make the calls to my family. 'Hello... I... I... have some really really bad news... Abigail... Abigail... was... she was... in a car accident last night... in Castletown and... she died' my voice trembling. I heard my sister Vicky scream; unable to speak to me. Barry her husband came on the phone and asked what's happened. I just blurted 'Abigail's been in an accident and she died.' My voice breaking, trying to hold back the tears, I continued 'look after Vicky for me please.' I put the phone down and sobbed. I wanted to be with my sisters. I still hear their screams in my head, the gasps of air and their cries. I repeated this over and over again that morning. Calling my family was unbelievably difficult, but I had to do it.

I became numb inside. I would sit and sob after each call, helpless. I wanted to scream but didn't. I would call the next number and have the exact same conversation over and over again. I spent most of that morning on the phone. Sitting in the hallway, the third step up, now known as Abigail's stair. I wanted to go and get her and bring her home. I so wanted this all to be wrong, for someone to come and tell me it wasn't Abigail, they'd made a mistake.

I wanted to go back in time, rewind those few hours so I could see her again, I wanted to stop her getting in that car, then it would all be alright.

Later that day our house became full. Friends were coming to help, to offer their condolences. It was lovely in its own way. Friends, family and neighbours were all there for us, coming and going. We were surrounded by people who loved and cared for us all. I can never thank them enough.

Our Police Family Liaison Officer, Ruth arrived at our home in the afternoon and introduced herself, she is a lovely kind caring lady. She talked us through certain things we had to do and asked us questions. Ruth also told us about the other passengers in the car who were injured, I was so worried about them, hoping that they would be alright. I couldn't stop thinking about them. I remember her giving me Abigail's possessions, everything in individual clear bags, it was heartbreaking. I took everything out of each bag and put them all back in Abigail's handbag. That's where her things were supposed to be, it's where they belonged. I gave Hannah Abigail's bracelet and I put her rings on. Surrounded by friends and family, the silence, the pain we all felt. No one wants to ever go through this.

Too many cups of tea! I think that's all we did that day; drink tea and eat biscuits. I HATE tea, I've never really been a fan but there is something comforting about holding a warm cup of tea filled with sugar and dunking biscuits.

Our friends Julie and Rab came over and told us that Ian and Bert, local fire fighters we know, both attended the scene of the accident. Ian, Bert and their families have all been family friends for many years. I used to work with Ian and often saw him jump into action to get to the fire station when his pager went off. I trust them both with my life and my daughter's. I felt a shooting pain in my heart, what they must have seen and the job they had to do that night. I felt for them. I am so grateful to them and all the rescue services for the fantastic work they do. I know if my daughter could have been saved, she would have been. They are fantastic and we take them all for granted.

I remember talking about funeral arrangements that day; we really didn't know what to do for the best. We lived in Scotland but are from Essex, where do we have Abigail buried? At first I thought she should be cremated so we could split her ashes in two and have a service in both. But this wasn't right and thankfully we came to the right decision to bury our daughter in the place where she loved to be, Thurso in Scotland. Abigail had told me just a few weeks earlier that she loved living in Scotland; she had so many friends, more than she had had anywhere else.

I thought I would never drive through Castletown again, never wanting to drive past the scene of the accident. Then later that day Julie called to tell me that flowers were already being left there for her. I had to go and see them. Weyland drove us, Paul in the front, my mum and I in the back. I felt sick, shaking inside, empty. It's not a very long journey but it seemed it that day. On the way Ruth called to ask if Abigail's name could be released to the press and we were told the names of everyone in the car. So much to take in, in such a short space of time.

We arrived in Castletown and parked at the roadside; it was sickening. This is where our daughter died, the last moments of her life ended here. I couldn't stand, my legs gave way, the pain in my chest hurt so much, I felt I was being crushed. I cried out and my Mum held me up to stop me from falling to the ground. Some of Abigail's friends arrived to leave flowers while we were there; it was obvious they felt uncomfortable. I could see they were unsure as to whether or not they should drive off and return later when we weren't there. I said it was Ok and waved them to come over. They came and hugged me; I think I just hung onto them. I stared at the young lad who drove them. I didn't know if this was the driver who had killed my daughter or not. So much pain and so many emotions to deal with. I just glared, wondering, feeling the anger well up inside me but I stayed where I was and said nothing.

We read the lovely messages her friends had left with their flowers. It was very touching. There were teddies, make-up, especially pink lip gloss; Abigail's favourite. She couldn't possibly have lived without her lip gloss. This meant so much to me and my family. I took a teddy left by her best friend Becca and I kept it with me all the time, I didn't want to let it go. I still keep it safe.

* * *

I was worried about Hazel, Abigail's friend who I knew very well. She'd been in the car with Abigail. I needed to know she was Ok. It must have been horrendous for her. I didn't want to know what happened and I didn't want Hazel to have to relive it to tell me. I just wanted to know that she was safe and that she was alright. Paul and I went to her home later that evening. She lived in the next street from us. I knocked on the door. I heard her call out in a panic.

'It's Abigail's Mum, it's Abigail's Mum.'

I saw her dad rush past her to open the door, I panicked and blurted 'I just want to give her a hug; I need to know she's Ok.'

Her dad let me past and I just stood there hugging Hazel, sobbing in each other's arms. We sat and talked with her and her parents. The relief that it wasn't their daughter didn't show, only the sorrow they felt for us. This could have so easily been the other way round.

I explained to Hazel that I will never ask her what happened, I will never make her relive that night but if she ever needed to talk, I would always be there for her.

'Life just isn't fair, it's fucking shit'

The drive to Inverness

It was now the early hours of Monday morning, less than thirty hours since I'd been told the worst news of my life. I'd had very little sleep, if any. I lay in bed awake. My body riddled with pain, my eyes sore. All that was going through my head was how on earth are Paul and I going to drive over a hundred miles to identify our daughter's body? How are we going to get through this?

My Mum was coming early to look after Hannah. Weyland had very kindly offered to drive us, but we wanted to be alone.

I couldn't sleep, tossing and turning. I didn't want to wake Paul, so I quietly crept out of bed and went downstairs. I didn't really know what to do with myself and wandered around aimlessly. I went into the dining room and saw the paint and brushes still lying there on the floor. I decided to start painting the edge of the feature wall. The paint was called "Espresso," a very dark brown against the cream walls. Inside I felt I was violently shaking. I just kept thinking "I can't do today. How can we possibly drive all that way?" So, in my head I talked to Abigail. I asked her to keep me strong, to help me. I thought, if I could paint a straight line while shaking and with the tears running, then I knew I could do anything. And so I did, I painted every stroke with her. At one point it felt as though she giggled and I giggled too. The blob on the wall is still there but as for the rest of the four edges, they were perfect. I did it, piece of cake, perfectly straight all done by hand with Abigail. I felt amazing. I could drive. I was so calm. It was completely surreal. Paul woke and was looking around the house for me. He looked really worried when he saw me. He said he was scared I had gone off and done something silly. 'No, just painting with Abigail!' I told him.

We drove in silence for almost two hours. I focused on driving safely and tried not to think about anything. I was numb. Eventually I turned the music on and broke the silence. Paul and I began to talk but I can't remember what about. Probably the weather, anything but what we were actually doing. We pulled up at the Police Headquarters in Inverness and met Ruth. She introduced us to the Investigating Officer from the Road Traffic Police, a nice gentleman. He told us that Scott the driver was very remorseful and so were his family. At this point we still didn't know what had happened and weren't ready to hear yet.

But thinking about Abigail's funeral I wasn't sure if the driver should be there or not, even if he wanted to. So I explained to the officer that if an animal or someone had run into the road and had caused the driver to swerve then I could accept him being there. But if he was driving recklessly and had caused this, then no he couldn't. That's when I think I was told there were two cars involved and that Scott was speeding. Decision made. The two drivers were not welcome.

Ruth received a call from the mortuary. They were waiting for us. Ruth drove us to Raigmore Hospital to identify Abigail's body. The emptiness inside; hollow. It was impossible to feel anything but numb, no emotions, just a vacant feeling of nothingness, life no longer existed inside me.

I told Ruth we had decided that Abigail could be an organ donor. I hadn't stopped thinking about it. Ruth then told us that she couldn't be. It was too late. Then it dawned on me, of course not. Her body had died, her organs no good to anyone. A tear ran down my cheek, I felt so sad. So many people could have benefited from her perfectly healthy body; she could have lived on within others. This wasn't to be. I have since decided that I am happy to donate all of me, take whatever is needed. This body of mine is just my shell.

We got out of the car and I felt myself shaking, trembling with fear, terrified of what we were about to see. As we walked slowly towards the door I began to panic, my chest felt so tight I was finding it difficult to breathe. I was being crushed from the inside. We went inside with Ruth and sat in the waiting room. Paul and I glanced at each other in silence, holding hands, unable to believe where we were. I told Ruth,

'I can't do this. You will have to use her dental records. I don't want to see her. I want to remember Abigail as I do now, before I walk through there' and pointed to the door. 'This memory will stay with me forever and I don't want it.'

Ruth offered to go in before us and come back and describe Abigail to us. I felt terrible that she had to go in, but I didn't know what else to do. When she returned she sat and calmly told us in detail what we were about to see. The room layout, where Abigail was and what to expect. We finally went in. Paul and I stood there in silence. Abigail lay in front of us with a purple blanket covering her just as Ruth had described. She was behind a glass screen, the right side of her face visible, her hair in such a mess, dried blood on her ear. This was my baby, my daughter. I wanted to protect her and keep her safe. But I hadn't; here she lay in front of me, dead, my baby. I couldn't touch her, I couldn't kiss her. I thought to myself that Scott, the driver of the car, the person that caused this, he should be standing here doing this, not me.

A very tall gentleman who seemed to be about seven foot tall came very quietly and stood by my side. He seemed like a gentle giant, very kind. He and the lady standing behind him were going to carry out the post-mortem. He read something to me and then read out Abigail's full name. They got it wrong, he said "Jane" instead of "Jade" in her middle name. I calmly repeated back to him 'Her name is Abigail Wendy-Jade Simpson.' He seemed very cross and corrected his paperwork. But I didn't care, it was right now. I stood there staring at Abigail in a daze. I had to say that this was her and sign his form.

Paul and I stood there silent for what felt like eternity. We were unable to move. Someone softly put their hand on my back and I knew it was time to leave. Paul and I looked at each other and left quietly. Ruth drove us back to our car where Paul and I just stood in the car park and held each other tightly.

Surprisingly we felt fine afterwards. Shock causes that. We think we're alright but really were not, of course not. How could we be? I can't believe it looking back that we then drove to my employer's regional office in Inverness, just round the corner from the police HQ. I asked if we could use a pc. I wanted to do two things. Firstly look up a social networking website. I'd received a text from Tammy, one of Abigail's friends to say that everyone was leaving messages for her. Secondly we needed to find the phone number of Dunnett's Funeral Directors who'd been highly recommended. I thought I wouldn't be able to call them when we got home late that night. I assumed they worked nine to five. I hadn't realised that in their profession they actually work twenty four hours a day, seven days a week: of course people pass away at any time of day or night, so they're always on call.

My colleague Miranda saw us first and took Paul and I into a quiet room and let us be. While there, I received a text from my Mum to say that my sisters, Lisa and Vicky were both flying to Inverness that afternoon. I couldn't wait to see them. I realised in that moment just how much I needed them both. It meant the world to me that they dropped everything and flew up to be with us.

When we finished using the internet we went upstairs to see my colleagues. Surprised to see us of course, they each gave Paul and I a hug. It's amazing the power and strength a hug gives, saying so much without a word being spoken.

We left and drove to the airport to meet my sisters. We hugged and cried. I was so pleased they were here.

I didn't have anything to wear to Abigail's funeral and thought this would be the only opportunity I would have to go shopping. Ridiculous I know but nobody knew us here, we were anonymous. We stopped at Next in Inverness Retail Park on our way back from the airport. This was more difficult than I thought. I walked around the store looking at clothes but with my mind totally elsewhere. Then it suddenly dawned on me, how on earth do I pick an outfit for my daughter's funeral? I stood in the middle of the shop and cried. I wanted to buy something to wear to her wedding not her funeral. That's what parents are supposed to do.

I didn't want to wear all black. I tried on several different outfits but nothing felt right. But then of course nothing probably would. My sisters went backwards and forwards selecting different things for me to try on. Staff and customers coming and going, I ignored everyone, my head down, no eye contact with anyone except Lisa and Vicky.

My friend Maggie called me, she had missed my call. I sat slumped in the changing room. So pleased to hear her voice, but also reliving that same conversation over again. This was never going to end. Abigail had died. I came off the phone, not really interested in trying anything else on.

One more change of clothes and finally we found the right one, smart black trousers and a lovely cream jacket. I decided I was going to wear a pink corsage on the day which felt more appropriate for Abigail. It was lovely for me to have my sisters with me to help. This couldn't have been easy for them; they were grieving for their niece and watching their sister go through hell.

My stepsister Catherine was the first to send flowers - beautiful white roses had been delivered to my mum for me. When we arrived home Elspeth had left a bag on our doorstep; everyday essentials, so very thoughtful and just what we needed.

'Abigail I want you to come home; to hold you once more,

to kiss you and tell you as I always did,

just how much I love you'

Cards and Flowers

Among the first of many flowers to arrive at our home were some from Wick Girl Guiding district. I've loved being involved in Girl Guiding within the county. I've held many different roles from Rainbow leader to Centenary Champion. Eleanor, the Wick District Commissioner had arranged for a beautiful pink flower arrangement to be delivered to us. I was so touched, for me it was so unexpected.

Then the flowers just kept on arriving, one after the other. So many. It was a very emotional time and I couldn't believe everyone's kindness. There was a constant stream of bunches and beautiful arrangements being delivered; friends, family, colleagues and even STV News.

I bumped into lots of Abigail's friends in the street. One young lad asked me to wait there with his friends. He ran off and came back a few moments later with a bunch of pink roses. Such a beautiful thought, he touched my heart. It meant the world to me.

Our house filled with their scent; the living room full, they covered every inch of our kitchen, no room to make all those cups of tea. I quickly ran out of vases. Instead of asking our new neighbours for a few spoons of sugar or a cup of milk, I was knocking asking if they had vases I could borrow! I love flowers and didn't want to end up hating their look and smell. I didn't want their scent to be a memory of this time. I contacted the florists to ask 'Could they let people know to stop sending us flowers please? We are grateful but can't cope with how many we have.'

They offered to keep them on hold for me; I could have them when I was ready. Not thinking straight I remember saying 'But they will all die by the time I'm ready for them, our house is full.'

They explained it was alright; they would keep the order on hold and deliver the card. I could have the arrangements made weeks or months later when I was ready. Perfect.

Nearly a week later some of the flowers began to wilt, I started to remove the dying flowers and began to cry, I couldn't bear to see them. This brought so much pain; it was like watching Abigail die in front of me. Over the next few days Paul and I decided to give all the flowers away to Pentland View Nursing Home just round the corner from us. They were delighted. Paul and I took two car trips to deliver them all and it really brightened their home.

My friend Sheilagh from the Kiln Store very kindly gave Paul and I a memory foam pillow each instead of flowers. She said she thought they might help us sleep. It was such a wonderful gift.

The florist cards continued to be delivered. It wasn't until some weeks later that I went to find out what I had to collect. Shocked, I discovered between the two florists in town I had almost three hundred pounds worth of flowers waiting for me. Both shops offered us the monetary value instead if I preferred and could choose whatever I wanted. I ordered an artificial arrangement to be made for Christmas to fit in with the colour scheme of my dining room; I love it and use it throughout the year, not just for Christmas. I don't see them as Abigail's funeral flowers, just Abigail's flowers. I adore them along with the willow and other artificial flowers I had purchased. I even took up flower arranging classes and used the money for this too. We had fresh flowers and arrangements in our home every month; right up until Abigail's first anniversary when I spent the remainder of what was left. Flowers for a whole year! It was amazing and I loved them all.

* * *

There were also hundreds of sympathy cards being delivered, so many that our postie put an elastic band round them to keep our normal mail and cards separate. I counted nearly thirty in just one day. I used to sit on what I call "Abigail's step," the one I sat on to tell everyone about the accident, the third step up. I continued to sit there every time I had to deal with the police and Victim Support, in fact anything to do with Abigail I sat on that stair. It's funny in my home now, when dealing with anything stressful, I still sit on the third step up.

There were so many cards with kind messages for us, some from complete strangers. They had heard through the media, both local and national newspapers and on STV news. Some days it was difficult to cope with everyone's kind words or their memories of Abigail. Cards and letters arrived from all over the world. Abigail's friends on holiday when they heard the news had sent a card from there thinking of us. Friends who had moved abroad had heard the news and sent their condolences; it was remarkable and so very touching.

I didn't know what to do with them all, cards were everywhere. My Mum asked,

'Do you plan to decorate the hallway?'

'Yes, one day' I replied.

'You could put them up on the wall there' she suggested.

And so I did, they filled every inch of my hallway from floor to ceiling but I remember saying as I blue tacked each one 'How on earth do I take these down?'

I later decided they could come down when I was ready to paint and wallpaper. We walked past the cards everyday and I actually liked them being there. Every so often I would take one or two down and sit on Abigail's step to read them. The most painful were from Abigail's friends detailing their memories, their sadness. I would sit holding the cards tightly to my chest, sobbing. The pain went so deep, their kind words so touching. Friends would come to our home and sometimes ask 'Is it time to take them down now?'

'No, not yet,' would be my reply.

Did it really matter how long they were there? I wasn't ready. Paul and Hannah didn't mind them; they didn't want to take the cards down either. So they stayed.

It was about six months before we were ready to decorate. By then the cards had become like our wallpaper and I missed them, but it was the right time for us. I bought a set of three lovely red and black velvet boxes to store them all in; the boxes sat stacked in my living room, everybody's love close by.

'Kindness touches the centre of your heart'

Message on the beach

A few of Abigail's friends came to see us at home on the Tuesday morning following the accident. We sat in her room and talked about their memories. We looked through her makeup and things. It was lovely to see her friends. They asked what they should wear to the funeral. I told them whatever they wanted to, they didn't have to wear black. More important for Abigail would have been that they took the time to get ready, to do their makeup and use their hair straighteners. They asked if they could wear pink. I thought this was perfect; Abigail would have loved the idea.

In between sobbing and sleeping I would wake up wanting to go to the beach to write Abigail's name really big in the sand, something we used to do as a family in Scotland when the girls were smaller. Although we lived right on top of Thurso beach we loved to drive to Melvich about sixteen miles from our home, to a beautiful idyllic beach that we always had all to ourselves. We would see footprints in the sand but no one ever there. It's a lovely drive to get there, along the country roads with of course the exception of the view of Dounreay Nuclear Power Station with its dome and office buildings. But even that's not so offensive to look at for the few brief minutes it takes to pass.

We would arrive near the beach and all clamber out of the car, kitted out in walking boots and winter clothes. We would all climb up the sand dunes, Paul and the girls performing slalom skiing jumps to go down the other side with me being a wimp walking down sideways, frightened I was going to fall. We would rush onto the beach and write our names in the sand and make sand angels. They were always big enough for us to see from the cliff top. We loved to go to the beach whatever the weather. We would often turn up at our friends Maggie and Iain's house on our way home wrapped in warm winter clothes with hat, scarf and gloves for a cup of tea. I first met Maggie when we both worked for Manpower at British Telecom. Maggie and Iain are both more than friends, they're family to me. Maggie would always say as she opened the door,

'You haven't all been to the beach again? It's freezing out there!'

In Caithness if you wait for sunbathing weather to arrive you might only get a glimpse of the beach once each year. The sun often shines but it's generally windy, and cold with it. Caithness has a beautiful landscape that most people would dream of living near. Some of the most stunning beaches I have ever seen are in Caithness and Sutherland, our neighbouring county. If the weather was hot the scenery would no doubt be spoilt by huge hotels. So I love the cold weather, it keeps people away! I can have my own private beautiful beach all to myself - selfish I know.

I asked Abigail's friends if they would like to help me write her name on Thurso beach and arranged to meet them there the following day. I wanted to write it really big and cover it in pebbles. I told them I would find out the tide times; all her friends were welcome to join us.

I sent just one text message to Hazel to say what time we were meeting and asked her to spread the word for me. The ripples had started.

Later that afternoon and evening more and more of Abigail's friends came to see us. They were grieving too and I don't think they really knew what to do, they just wanted to be with us and so our house was full. Everywhere I looked there was someone. It was lovely to see so many of her friends. I found this comforting and amazingly I seemed to be coping Ok. But later, as the girls were sitting in the living room chatting, I flipped. I was angry with Scott. I didn't even know what he looked like. One of the girls showed me a picture of him on her phone. I asked them what I would have thought of him last week, before this all happened. I knew I wouldn't have hated him. I just sat there quiet, and then said out loud that I wanted a bottle of wine. I meant to say glass, but I drank a bottle. It felt good at the time, helping me to relax but of course later I felt awful. I had said things I wish I hadn't and my head was really sore. I understood very early on that alcohol was not going to help; in fact it would send me the other way. I felt so down and depressed it made me feel worse. I couldn't focus.

I craved a cigarette. I had given up smoking six years earlier and knew I didn't want to start again. A few people said Abigail wouldn't have wanted me to, but to be honest that really didn't help. I knew that I would regret it. When I gave up smoking the thought of not having a cigarette for the rest of my life, even twenty four hours terrified me. So in my head I only gave up for five minutes and by the time five minutes had passed I didn't want one. This worked for me then and I've never looked back, so I used this method again and never touched a cigarette, not one!

As the night went on I said it looked like we were having a party; so many youngsters, but Abigail was missing. She would have loved having so many of her friends over. I'm so glad they all came, it's like they kept Abigail alive that little bit longer, sharing so many happy memories.

A few weeks or months later my close friend Maria who we bought our house from told me that she had specifically told her son Liam not to come and see us. She had said that we needed to be alone with our family. Liam was Abigail's first serious boyfriend, they were only thirteen. It was always lovely to see them walking down the road holding hands, not embarrassed if we saw them. I always had a soft spot for Liam; he is a lovely cheeky lad who would always make me laugh. He will hate me for saying that! Maria told me how he had come home that night and said 'It's alright, Abigail's mum's Ok.' I told her he was right to come round. I really needed the kids around me. they helped to keep me strong and they kept me close to Abigail as I probably did them.

When I arrived at the promenade the following morning there were a group of girls waiting. I didn't recognise them but by the way they were looking at me I guessed they were there for us. I walked over and said 'Hi, have you to come to help?' The girls attempted to smile and nodded. I thanked them and explained that we would wait for the others to arrive. I hovered with Paul and Hannah not wanting to make them feel awkward around us.

We waited, then suddenly from both directions there were so many of Abigail's friends walking towards us. We weren't really sure what to do so I said that Hannah and I would write our message. They could all come down onto the beach and put the pebbles on each of the letters to make them stand out.

Hannah and I walked down the steps and onto the beach. Using a broom handle we started to write our message: "Abigail We Love You X X" with the word 'Love' represented by a huge heart in the sand. We put two kisses because Abigail always put two at the end of her text messages to me. I waved for her friends to join us as we carried on writing. Hannah went to join her friends laying the pebbles one by one. As I looked around I couldn't believe just how many were there; masses and masses of youngsters, Abigail's friends. Those that loved and cared for her and missed her too. When I looked up at the promenade it was full of adults, their parents, friends and passersby; all watching us. The esplanade was full.

Abigail was a very popular young girl. She was liked by so many, very laid back with a carefree attitude to life. Always bubbly and having fun, which is what I think attracted so many to her.

Paul had already told me he didn't want to come onto the beach. I think it would have been too painful for him. He stood and took photos which I'm so pleased he did as I treasure them now.

Each time I walked up and down the beach collecting pebbles I thanked those around me for coming and helping. This meant so much to them too, it gave us all purpose. I realised that although I needed to do this, it helped us all. My message was from each and every one of us. I hugged so many of Abigail's friends that day, they probably needed this just as much as I did; we were all connected to Abigail.

I was amazed at how they individually chose their stones, each one hand selected especially for Abigail, not just any pebble, they actually walked around looking for specific ones; it was wonderful. I noticed that they would stop and hug each other; this was such a beautiful experience. As we laid the last of the pebbles on the outline of the letters they started to gather and slowed down. I looked around and said 'We haven't finished, we need to fill her heart; Abigail never had an empty heart.' They all started to rush to get more stones. I laid the last ones and broke down and cried. I just sat there for a few moments with her friends all around me.

I heard someone say 'No we don't need any more, Abigail's mum has put the last ones down, put them back.'

I got up and went over to the young girl, I took one of the pebbles from her and said 'We will do it together.'

I put my arm around her and said to everyone that we should go up the steps and look down to see our message.

Wow. It was massive. I hadn't realised just how enormous it was. Each letter was huge. The heart itself was so big that when a photo of it was on the front page of the local paper a couple were standing by the side of it, they looked so small in comparison. Everyone was mingling together. Some had already left as they were late for college or had to go to work. Those that were at school could stay because it was half term holidays. I hugged and thanked them all.

People; friends and strangers were arriving to come and see our message on the beach and to offer their condolences to us. The group started to grow into a larger circle when one of them called me over for a "Group hug." Before we knew it all of Abigail's friends were joined in the hug. My mum, both my sisters along with Hannah and I joined them. I counted them all, over a hundred of us, all together, each of us missing Abigail. I felt so amazed, my daughter had touched each and every one of them. I am so proud to be the only person in the whole world who can say 'I'm Abigail's Mum.'

I later heard that the radio was broadcasting on the news that we had written our message on the beach and had apparently built a cairn! A cairn is a Scottish Gaelic word for a stack or pile of stones. Cairn's can be found all over the world but ours was our love heart. So many people were texting me to say how lovely it was. People were actually going out of their way to go there to see it. I didn't realise the impact this would have, this wasn't my intention. It was just my personal message to Abigail that grew to a message of love from us all.

That evening before dark I wanted to go and see it again and hoped that it would be washed away by the morning. I was worried that if any remained, Abigail's friends might go and keep filling it in. It was our message for one day only.

As we arrived I saw friends, colleagues and neighbours who had come to see. I hugged them and asked if they wanted to lay a pebble on Abigail's heart. We went down onto the beach for each of them to place their pebble.

We stood there looking out to sea and listening to the waves. It was a typical dark night. The tide came in and we could hear the pebbles crashing and rolling against each other, it was a beautiful sound.

Hazel came running over to ask if she could take her pebble as she wanted to keep it. Hazel, Susan and Tammy had written "Love You Doll" along with their names on a large heart shaped stone they had found and placed in the centre on the heart. Of course it was Ok. They were going out so we offered to take it home with us, they could pick it up the next day. She never came to collect it, I can only assume it was either too much of a painful memory or she didn't want to take it from me. I guess the latter. It sat by our front door until we moved to Cyprus, their names have worn away. The stone now sits in my Mum's garden in safe keeping.

We stood on the promenade for a while listening to the sea. It was surreal, very peaceful and calm. I drove past the next morning, our message was gone; it was front page news by Friday morning in the local newspaper.

'Abigail We ♥ You X X'

Text Messages

Abigail's mobile phone was given back to us by the police without the battery in it, I can only assume because it was ringing in the car while they were carrying out their investigation.

I hated sitting at home staring at the same four walls, wandering from room to room not knowing what to do. Paul, Hannah and I all needed to get out of the house so we went for a drive. Nowhere to go in particular Paul just drove us out of Thurso and headed towards Wick, music on in the background, the three of us with our own thoughts, silent. We had no idea really what to say to each other. We were all grieving in different ways, emotions and feelings, memories all hidden away from each other. My thoughts continuously of Abigail. No room for anything or anyone else.

I knew Abigail had lots of photos and music stored on her phone. I wanted to see it all. I reached into my handbag and put her Sim card into mine to see if it would work. It started beeping, a text message had arrived, and then another and another. Without thinking I opened the text. It was from one of her friends saying that they loved her, another they missed her, texts were coming in thick and fast. All sent after they had heard about the crash. Messages of love; missing her.

I read three or four messages. I looked up and couldn't see, my eyes filled with tears, my heart broken.

I didn't read anymore, they weren't for me. They were sent privately to Abigail, things her friends wanted to say to her, the last thing they could and needed to do. Their last message to Abigail.

If only she knew how much she meant to us all.

'Communication is a wonderful thing'

A Special Moment

Exactly a week after the accident I needed to return to Castletown to where she'd died. I was told after the post-mortem that Abigail passed away at approximately nine thirty pm. I needed to light a candle for her. I wanted to be close to Abigail.

Lindsay came to look after Hannah for us as she didn't want to come. Lindsay, a close family friend, has been a great help and support to us over the years.

It was quite a windy evening so trying to keep one candle alight was tricky let alone all fifteen, one for every year of her life. I lit the first one. A couple walked passed us and bowed their heads. As I lit the second the first blew out. A tear ran down my cheek. I wanted to light them all. I tried again and the other blew out. This time I laughed and saw the funny side. I thought to myself "This is going to be impossible."

Cars drove past us extremely slowly; paying their respects. Eventually Paul and I had managed to light all fifteen, some hidden among the flowers but all alight. We walked across the road, sat on the dry stone dyke wall and watched them. I whispered to Paul that I wanted to wait until they had all blown out. We sat and watched huddled together, alone with our thoughts. One by one the candles went out but one stayed bright all alone for a long time, it didn't seem possible. I asked Paul what the time was, 9.38pm, it blew out a minute later. It was so surreal.

'Beautiful signs of Love'

Social Networking

The day after the accident, pages were set up in Abigail's memory on a social networking website. All her friends were leaving messages of love and sharing their memories of her. There were that many messages it even made the news! I read the messages time and time again. They made me smile and they made me cry; proud of my daughter and sad to be without her. After Abigail's funeral there were over ten thousand messages of love for her, condolences from all over the world, strangers who had never met her were leaving loving kind messages too.

I have asked a few of Abigail's friends to share their memories with you here as I wanted you to see a tiny glimpse of the kind of person Abigail was.

Jo Mancini

Abigail was one of those girls who was loved by everyone. I'll never forget her first day at Thurso high school, everyone getting excited in English class because there was a new girl. She always looked so perfect, her hair always immaculate, her makeup always done to perfection and her nails always perfectly manicured!

But the day I always remember and makes me laugh was the day Abigail didn't have any lipgloss! It was like sitting in an exam and not having revised for it! I sat behind

Abigail so I always looked forward to hearing her chat from the weekend. She turned around to me and said 'OMG I have no lipgloss please say you have some!'

Thankfully I did but it was this strange lip plumping gloss. I passed it over and explained 'you know Abigail it will tingle so don't worry if you feel like your lips are getting hot!' I spoke to soon, normally with this lipgloss it would tingle for a few minutes but with Abigail she was having an allergic reaction! Watching her trying to remove this was probably one of the funniest things I have ever seen in my life!!

Frantically trying to wipe it and lick it off smudging it all over her English book! Still makes me laugh to this day. And all she said after was.... 'Jesus I felt like my lips were gonna blow up, can I have some more?'

Now whenever I put on lip plumping gloss I always think of this special memory.

Becca

Five years of our friendship is one happy blur, from the sleepovers in the holidays that would last 4 days straight. Spending hours pouring over the Argos book so she could pick her birthday presents from every family member even if her birthday was 6 months away to sitting in modern studies listening to her daily changing future life plans, she was without a doubt one of kind and I'm lucky to have so many happy memories xxx

Mike

My lasting memory is you having a good laugh at my expense, when I ran across the road and tried to front flip over the railings and landed on my head. R.I.P sweetie, am sure you will be looking down smiling over us all... xxx

Sarah

Memories..... eeeekkk, trying to do a few lines is impossible.

I remember every time we were on a sleepover I used to always fall asleep before Abigail and she would sing aloud to her phone dancing in the bed, so one day I deleted the song on my phone so she couldn't play it Over and Over again, but I had to get it back for her!

Also, one time she got over exited when she woke up pretending to make a commercial advert for cornflakes for the telly. She woke me up jumping on the bed and singing whilst pulling the covers off me and opening the curtains. She kept repeating this till she got it perfect and I was awake laughing!!

I could go on with loads of little memories, everyone was a good one as we were always laughing when we were together!! But the best time was that summer we had when she came to mine in Essex and we went to Southend. We had a good laugh there, we kept going off giggling, getting on all the rides, getting up to mischief.

It's horrible to think that these memories seem soooo long ago, but her smile and laugh I can still picture. I can truly say there wasn't a single "bad time" I had with Abigail! We never once argued. I know that we would have had soooo many more great times and I hate the fact she is not hear with us anymore.

'It's good to share how you feel, it shows you care'

Funeral Arrangements

George and Sinclair Dunnett of Dunnett's Funeral Directors came to visit us at home to attend to Abigail's funeral arrangements; they were and are so lovely. Sinclair and his family have since become very close friends of ours. I had no idea what to expect, having heard stories in the past of funeral directors guilt-tripping you into buying the most expensive coffins. Seems ludicrous but you hear that it happens, so I'd prepared myself for this. I didn't need to, Dunnett's don't work like that at all. They're a very kind family who provide a wonderful service and make sure everything you choose is perfect for you.

I wasn't sure where to have Abigail's funeral, we didn't attend church, we're not religious people but a humanist service didn't seem right either. Abigail's service was held in St Peters and St Andrews Church in Thurso, the largest church in town. George Dunnett had said he expected there to be lots of people and we needed the biggest venue and a church did seem more appropriate for us. George and Sinclair listened to everything we said and made all the necessary arrangements for us, nothing was too much trouble. I needed this to be right for Abigail. A "Celebration of her Life."

I remembered years earlier watching the film "Love Actually" and saying to Abigail that if I knew I was dying I would do the same as the lady who had organised a projection of photos of her life to music. So, I decided that I wanted to do this for Abigail. I got the box of photos from the living room and took them all out. I laid favourites across the floor, there were so many. I wasn't sure which ones to choose and left them out covering the carpet. It was nice when Abigail's friends and our family came to see us as everyone looked at them and talked about Abigail. All sharing their happy memories.

When Paul and Hannah drove my sisters back to Inverness airport I spent the day at the computer scanning pictures and making a PowerPoint slideshow of Abigail's life. It was tough, but I needed to do it. At that time it was the last thing I felt I could do for her.

Friends of Abigail's had brought photos round as well, some taken on the afternoon of the day she died. They told stories of what they had all been up to at the shops. I kept putting one of the photos in my slideshow and would take it out again as I wasn't coping very well with it. The last day of her life, too much to bear. I wasn't with Abigail when the last photo of her was taken. The pain was too immense, seeing it cut so deep within me. I didn't want to see it; looking at it made me feel sick, the pain in my heart was physically impossible to live with. That's when I decided that this was "My fifteen years with Abigail." I was sharing my memories and favourite photos of her, so I didn't put it in. There were photos ranging from when she was born, funny ones when Abigail and Hannah were in the back of the car, holding bananas like they were telephones and making up all these silly conversations. I included Christmas photos, family holidays and days out, all that were special to me. I set the slideshow up to the song "You're Beautiful" by James Blunt.

It was perfect. I played it over and over again, the tears ran, I sobbed. Heartbroken. I have no idea how many boxes of tissues I got through. I still have the presentation stored on my laptop, every so often I will watch it. Sometimes it makes me smile and sometimes it makes me cry. Whatever the emotion it's Ok, it's good to remember.

It took me years to deal with the photo of Abigail that was taken the day she died. I would take it out of the drawer and look at it, cry, wipe my eyes and put it back. Not quite ready to have it out on display, a reminder too painful to have continuously in front of me. I kept looking at it, I was sure that one day it would get easier and eventually the day came when I put it in a frame and set it on the table. It's still there. I glance over and sometimes feel my heart sink and there are times when it makes me smile. A reminder of just how beautiful my daughter was inside and out.

* * *

We met with minister Murray Campbell from the Fishermans Mission and talked through what we would like for Abigail's service. Having never met us or Abigail before I am so pleased that George Dunnett had recommend Murray. I felt as though he knew us all. In just a short space of time Murray prepared the perfect service for her. It was beautiful. Stories of Abigail written by her friends were read along with Abigail's poem "Blue Bubbles." She wrote it when she was ten years old and showed it to her school teacher at Hilldene Primary when we lived in Essex. Her teacher entered it in the Hullabuloo competition. Abigail along with many other lucky children won and had their poems published.

A "Fingerprints" poem was read out as part of her service too. Abigail had made a calendar at playschool when she was about two or three. She painted her hands and printed them onto paper. The staff had then stuck them with the fingerprints poem and made them into calendars. I remember crying when she brought it home back then. I loved it and had it framed. I liked it so much that I made the same with Hannah when she was little and with my Brownies when I was a Brownie Leader. Abigail's was on display at her funeral in the church.

I asked if Craig Omand, Abigail's head of year and Modern Studies teacher would speak at Abigail's service. He had said such lovely things about Abigail at her last parents evening and I felt it was appropriate.

Craig Omand told stories of Abigail and her antics at school from being like road runner trying to cross the school hallway when the students were not allowed, to her trousers not quite covering all that they should. I knew this meant her thong was showing hence the boys were unable to pay attention in class. I moaned at her all the time about it but she would just huff then laugh and pull her trousers up. Craig made us smile.

George Dunnett and Murray Campbell came to see us on the Friday morning to confirm the funeral arrangements. I said that I had no idea what to really expect or how to cope with this and so Paul and I went with them to the church to where Abigail would be and where we would walk from and sit. Just to get our bearings and so I didn't have to worry on the day. I couldn't have asked for more, they had everything under control and had worked out where and how to project my photos.

Abigail's friends had said they would be taking pink balloons to let go in the cemetery. When I spoke to George and Murray about this they said that they wouldn't be appropriate in the church because people wouldn't be able to see. So they arranged to have a minibus go to the shop and collect all the balloons for everyone. I asked the shop to keep all those that were ordered for Abigail and if they minded explaining to people that their balloon would be at the cemetery for them when they arrived. Nothing was too much trouble for anyone. Dunnett's also arranged to get permission from the coastguard and airport control on the day to let them go. It's a good job they did because I would never have thought of it.

I had said to George and Sinclair that I didn't like funeral cars, those large black limousines always made me feel so sad whenever I saw people in them. They were obviously going to a close family member's funeral. I didn't want to get in one and decided that we would drive ourselves to church.

Sinclair was getting Abigail ready and we had chosen her clothes for her - white leggings and a silver dress. When we took them to their office we saw a large black Rover sitting outside. I asked if it was a funeral car. They said I could have that one if I wanted and so we did. It didn't look like a funeral car, in fact it turns out it was usually used for weddings. I could cope with that.

Later that day George called us to say Abigail was ready for us to see. Hannah went to Becca's Mum's instead as she didn't want to come with Paul and I. I was so nervous, more nervous now than when I had driven to identify her body. This was going to be the last time I saw my daughter. I was worried in case she didn't look like I remembered her.

Once again, just like before, I was shaking inside. I couldn't stop this horrible feeling. I have never felt so sad in all my life, so physically drained, so numb and helpless. George and Sinclair came to meet us at the entrance. We gave them a pair of earrings we wanted Abigail to wear. Paul had bought her new ones, the same as those she was wearing the night she died that we didn't get back.

I asked if I could kiss her and George explained that she would be very, very cold and suggested that I touched her with the back of my hand first. We slowly walked in. There was music playing softly in the background and we walked up to Abigail's casket. She looked like Abigail as I knew her. But Abigail wasn't there, her spirit had left. I felt this was her shell left behind. I touched her cheek like George said. She was really cold, not icy cold but just cold, like nothing I've ever touched before. I kissed my fingers and placed them on her cheek, a tear ran from eye, this was my baby lying here and I had to say goodbye.

* * *

Before Abigail's funeral I kept returning to Castletown to read all the messages and collect the lovely cards and gifts that were being left for her. They included teddies, makeup, mascara, lip glosses, a bracelet and a purse along with so many flowers. At first I didn't know what to do with all the gifts. I didn't want to keep them all, they weren't for me. In the end I decided to put them in a lovely gift bag and gave them to Abigail. These gifts were for her and so they have been buried with her.

When my sisters arrived back in Caithness for the funeral they asked if they could go and see her. I said no initially because I didn't want to have to go again, I wanted to be the last person to see her, I'm her Mum. But on the morning of Abigail's funeral I woke really early and wanted to see her again, this was my last chance. I called Sinclair and asked if we could. He agreed but said we had to be there soon. I called all my family to let them know if they wanted to go they had to get up and get ready now. We met them there a while later. Each one went in turn to see her. Paul and I went last and said bye to our Abigail once more.

Later that morning our family were arriving at our home to leave for the funeral service with us. Susan from Dunnett's funeral directors came to drive us to the church. She checked we were all Ok and to see how we were coping. I asked if the media were there. Abigail's passing had been on the front page of several local newspapers and on STV news but I didn't want them there, this was private. She said she hadn't seen them. She told us where we would be going and what to do. Susan looked after us. My sister Vicky said to me it was like being around a celebrity with all the uncertainty of media coverage. Only we're not celebrities and don't want to be. But Abigail did.

Abigail was taken straight to St Peter's and St Andrews church. Dunnett's sent a minibus to our home to collect our friends and family. Susan drove Paul, Hannah and I. When we arrived we were taken to the back entrance to walk in from there. George anticipated it would be too overwhelming for us to sit in church and wait for everyone to arrive. From his experience he expected there to be people in their hundreds. He suggested that our close friends and family wait in the back area of the church where they could be with us while everyone else arrived and we would all walk in together. I couldn't believe there were so many close friends and family there. I kissed and hugged everyone. I was shocked to see some of our friends and family had flown up to Scotland to be with us, I hadn't expected them. Their support meant the world to us. I couldn't sit so I stood with Susan. She had my box of tissues. I knew I would need them; a small packet was nowhere near enough.

I felt numb as we slowly walked into church following George. I gently tugged at the back of his jacket, 'Slow down' I whispered as I struggled to walk close behind him. I felt like he was shielding me from everything and everyone. He was my protector and even now when in George's company I always feel safe.

The church was full. I only saw a few people, my head bowed, too sad to even lift my head. Sinclair later told me there was somewhere between five and six hundred people at the service. Incredible! My daughter had touched so many throughout her short life and to our surprise so many of our colleagues from all over the country had travelled to be there. It was and is amazing to look back on. I am so proud of my daughter and my family.

Funerals in Scotland are different to any I'd been to in England. I hadn't realised that people would be waiting outside the church to see us before we left for the cemetery. The streets were lined with people. I stopped in my track as I approached the church doors to leave with Paul and Hannah by my side. It took my breath away when I saw them. I didn't know how to move.

George very softly said to me 'It's alright, take your time.'

I didn't want to see anyone. I thought everyone would have already left. I struggled to look anyone in the eye. We got in the car and Susan drove us to the cemetery. I remember all the traffic stopped at the traffic lights to allow the cars to pass. There were so many and they all waited patiently. As we drove past the roadwork's outside the supermarket all the workers stopped, took off their hard hats and bowed their heads to the hearse; to Abigail and then to us. I felt so touched by their actions, their kindness.

We passed a young girl walking to the cemetery carrying her pink high heels. This made me laugh. I pointed her out to Hannah and Paul and said,

'Abigail would have done that too!'

We all smiled and talked about Abigail. I recall Susan telling us she would get into trouble with George for laughing. He was in the hearse in front and would see her in his interior mirror. I told her this was right for us, we should remember happy times. I needed to. I didn't want to be burying my daughter.

When we arrived at the cemetery Susan explained that we should wait in the car as lots of Abigail's friends were walking and hadn't taken the offer of the minibuses. Crowds of them all walked together and we needed to give them time to arrive.

Once ready George guided us to Abigail's grave. I didn't want to stand at the end and asked if we could move. We were surrounded by hundreds of people. It was tough holding it together. So many of Abigail's friends had carried pink balloons. I had ordered some for friends and family who had travelled to Caithness and at the end of the service everyone stood holding their balloons. George handed me mine. I just stared at it. Eventually I looked up at George and said 'I don't know if I can let it go.' My eyes filled and slowly the tears ran down my cheeks. I felt I had to let go of Abigail, but I didn't want to, I didn't know how to.

George very kindly whispered,

'Would you like me to get a pair of scissors to cut it for you?'

I smiled. He knew me so well already. Everyone started to release their balloons. I couldn't watch. I looked at the ribbon in my hand. The tears rolled down my face. Then slowly I began to release my thumb and forefinger and watched the ribbon glide through my hand. I gasped for air. I'd been holding my breath so tightly. I looked up to watch my balloon rise high into the sky; it was incredible to see them all floating up, so many altogether.

George whispered to me, 'Like blue bubbles, only pink' he was referring to Abigail's poem read earlier at the service.

I smiled and watched as the balloons slowly drifted in the direction of where we used to live in Spittal.

I turned and hugged some of our close friends, two of them Ian and Bert, the fire fighters who were at the scene of the accident. It was difficult to see them, imagining what they must have seen, what they had to go through and here they were at her funeral. I hugged Ian and Bert so tightly I didn't want to let them go. I wanted to thank them.

As we left the cemetery my Aunt Lyn waved to stop our car and pointed to the sky. There was a beautiful rainbow stretching right across all the houses in front of us. It was amazing.

We went to the British Legion in Thurso afterwards for tea, sandwiches and cake, not that I had any. I was shown to our table in the middle of the room. I couldn't and didn't sit there. I wandered off and mingled. I needed to be among everyone. I moved from table to table and heard how lovely they all thought the service was while they shared happy memories of Abigail.

It was wonderful to see how smart all the kids looked. They all wore pink and black, even the boys, who wore either a pink shirt or a pink tie. They looked smarter than when they went to school, they had all made such an effort. I really appreciate the time they had taken in purchasing something special to wear and making sure they all looked so smart and lovely. It added to making the day exceptional for us. They had shown in so many ways over the previous ten days just how much Abigail meant to them. They came together in unity and could support each other as well as us, although they probably didn't realise it.

That same afternoon a few of our friends who didn't to come to the British Legion went for a walk to reflect on the day at different locations and both saw a complete rainbow across the bay from where we lived in Scrabster to Castletown where Abigail died. It was there all afternoon and not a drop of rain in sight. "Abigail's Rainbow." My friend Lindsay took a photograph for us; it needed two pictures to capture the enormity of it. So many people where touched by the rainbow. Abigail shone above us all. It was incredible.

I was later told that people saw a full rainbow as they arrived at the cemetery too. Because we were in the car we were too low to see it and when I got out of the car my head was bowed, so I missed it.

My Aunt Lyn later told me that she also saw four angels in the clouds as she left the cemetery; she said 'Abigail was being buried in the Valley of the Rainbows.'

Later that evening her friends all got together on the beach and invited Paul, Hannah and I along with all our friends and family who were with us to join them. The boys lit a huge bonfire. Me, worrying as usual, asked Paul if he would join them. He didn't want to interfere, this was their thing, but he went down to chat to them and kept an eye on things. The rest of us sat on the wall with most of the girls on the promenade. It was such a lovely gesture and was nice to be included, to spend time with them all while we were all grieving wishing Abigail was here with us.

Blue Bubbles

Blue bubbles, blue bubbles
Blue bubbles everywhere
Blue bubbles in the garden
Blue bubbles up the stairs
Blue bubbles in the bathtub
Blue bubbles in the sea
Blue bubbles everywhere
Oh deary, deary me

Abigail Simpson aged 10

Craig Omand's Euology

'Thurso High School in the words of Dr Grant, Head of Thurso High School, has lost a very popular pupil. And as her classroom teacher and Year Head, I would also add a very likeable one with a keen sense of humour. She was even gracious enough to laugh at my pretty feeble classroom jokes. Now, I could tell everyone here that Abigail was an angel in everything she did. No one is an angel, not even my eight month old daughter who I of course adore. Abigail liked to push some boundaries just that wee bit, but she had a spirit in her which endeared many of her friends, fellow pupils and teachers towards her. If my daughter grows up to develop some of the qualities I believe Abigail had, I'll be more than happy.

Now this sounds a somewhat daft schoolteacherish thing to say, but my overriding image of Abigail was her unique ability to take a row. A Deputy Head has to discipline pupils as a regular part of their job. As Abigail's Year Head I had on occasion to have a word with her over classroom issues. Some pupils respond to a glower, some to a raised voice. Abigail was different. I taught Abigail Standard Grade Modern Studies. I'd have the class in task, working quietly and then... that unmistakable sound of whisper, whisper, whisper would at times be heard. I would see a neck slightly craned to her neighbour and an eye squinted towards the football pitch. My behaviour management tactic with her was to gently walk up and quietly say 'Can I help you ladies?'

Abigail would immediately say 'Sorry Sir!' and proceed to start writing at high speed in her workbook.

Similarly Mr Murphy, a man just occasionally associated with grumpiness often had reason to speak with Abigail each morning. The flagstone area inside the school entrance is closed to pupils at certain times of the day. Very often Abigail, a bit like an MI5 agent would scan to see if teachers were patrolling the area, and then bolt across to take a short cut to her Registration Class. Nine times out of ten Mr Murphy would apprehend her. It was a bit like the coyote in the Roadrunner cartoons, if at first you don't succeed, try, try again, even though you knew the chances of success were slim. Sometimes Mr Murphy hadn't even managed to say Abigail's name and she'd be replying 'Sorry Sir! and scurry back.

Abigail took a row with dignity and a maturity beyond her years. The life skill of how to diffuse a situation by being calm and polite is a quality not all adults possess, let alone a fifteen year old.

She was also particularly praised at her work experience placement in June for just these qualities.

Her Pupil Support teacher Mr McKeesick emphasised this when he mentioned a Dress Code issue he had to talk to Abigail about. Abigail consistently turned up to school immaculately groomed and took great pride in her appearance. However Mr McKeesick said to me 'I had to have a word wi' the lassie as her breeks (trousers) were no' covering everything they should.'

Again fair play to Abigail, she reported back the next day and asked 'Do you like my trousers Sir?' This fashion-consciousness was also remarked upon in an ICT lesson. The class was allowed the last five minutes to browse the internet. What was Abigail Googling? BBC News? The Modern Studies Association? No it was the Gucci and Prada Home pages she visited.

Thurso High had a third year parents' evening before the summer and when Paul and Nicola came to see me, they were pleased to report that she was progressing in many of her subjects. She had also reached the upper Credit level in my class. I wrote on her then assessment, 'Excellent effort. Your answer technique is maturing and you are developing a more convincing vocabulary to develop your points.' So even when she was having a fly look at a football match, she was actually still doing her best to work!

What her friends, fellow pupils and teachers shall retain about Abigail is a girl with a dignity, calmness, humour and an essential decency. The Simpson family can be justly proud of their daughter.

Abigail will be hugely missed by this community and the community school that Thurso High School is.

But she would undoubtedly want us all to leave this place with a smile on our face when we think of her.'

Thurso High School

Craig later informed me that the school wanted to have their own remembrance for Abigail after the half term holiday. He invited Paul, Hannah and I to attend.

They planted a pretty fuchsia in the garden, Abigail's favourite flower which was pink of course. Several of Abigail's close friends were invited to join us and helped plant it. We were asked back to one of the classrooms with her friends for tea and biscuits where they presented us with a memory book they had made for us. Many of her classmates had contributed to it telling us their funny stories, the things Abigail would say and do. It was beautifully presented in a lovely Paperchase album.

I will treasure all of their wonderful memories forever.

'I will always love you Abigail'

Torment

I would lie awake at night, the events of that night going over and over in my mind. Imagining the journey, what happened, what it must have felt like for Abigail and her friends?

What was going through her mind?

Was she aware Scott had lost control? Did she realise she was in danger?

Was she scared, afraid, did she panic? Was it all over instantly?

But you know some of the hardest questions too are: what was the last song she heard playing? Did she realise she had died? None of us really know about life after death. We all have our own opinions and feelings on the matter, but none of us actually know.

I remembered my pregnancy, how wonderful it felt to have Abigail growing inside me. My cravings for Cornetto ice cream, unable to decide which flavour to have, so I would buy all three. I would recall giving birth to her and trying my best as any parent does to protect their child throughout their life. I was there for all that, but I wasn't there at the end.

I had been responsible for Abigail her whole life. Until she sat in Scott's car, then she was his responsibility. He didn't look after her, he didn't protect her. He was there with her, along with her friends at the end of her life. I wasn't. I couldn't protect her and there was nothing I could do to save her.

I lay in bed with all these images flashing through my mind, all horrific, terrifying. Without answers, my imagination ran riot.

Angry, with so much hate boiling in my blood keeping me awake at night. I didn't want to kill Scott. I wanted to torture him. I wanted him to feel my pain. I wanted to stab him, starting with his hands and feet, working my way up his arms and legs, never getting to his body. I wanted him to live, to see my anger, the fury raging inside me, the hate in my eyes.

I imagined ducking him in water over and over again until he almost drowned, letting him up for small gasps of air until he was barely alive.

I then wanted to hang him by his feet and start a fire below his head to smell his skin melting; to hear him scream, then set him free and tell him that this pain was only a tiny glimpse of what I feel every second of every day.

I wanted to hurt him. The thoughts running through my mind were far worse than any horror movie I'd ever seen, the anger and rage bubbling away inside me.

Sometimes I would wake in the night wanting to go and grab him out of his bed and put him in my car and drive like mad. I wanted him to be terrified as I drove us both over a cliff. Kill us both. I didn't want to live anymore.

These feelings lasted months, eating away at me. I just couldn't get them out of my head. This was living hell, this wasn't me. I'm glad that phase has passed.

I know he is in pain, I know that he is sorry. He's not evil; he made a stupid, stupid mistake that has destroyed us all, his family and mine. I realise now that Scott must be suffering too.

'Causing pain and suffering will never bring her back'

Returning to Work

Near the end of October I thought I should start to think about going back to work even though it was only about three weeks after the accident. I couldn't stay at home all the time, it wasn't good for me. I needed the distraction.

I called my line manager and understood that she seemed surprised. We arranged a time for me to return about a week or so later. They were very supportive and fortunately they didn't really expect too much from me.

My job was to help people back into employment from different programmes. I worked with people from the age of sixteen right up to those almost retiring who had been out of work for some time. I would source work experience placements and support them back into the working environment. Through this, I knew a lot of people in our community from clients, employers, support agencies and schools to careers advisors all of whom I worked very closely with across Caithness and Sutherland areas.

In my head the first day back seemed alright, quite logical, but putting it into practice was a whole other board game. I got in my car and drove round the corner; I must have only travelled a few hundred meters from my home when I began to cry. Asking myself over and over again 'What are you doing?' But I decided to continue, I knew I wasn't ready deep down inside but I needed a focus, somewhere to go just to get me out of the house. I thought if I could drive the twenty odd mile journey to work then that would be a success and if I could sit at my desk and just stare at the screen then that would be a huge achievement.

Eventually I arrived at the office, the journey seemed to have taken forever. I walked in, everyone surprised to see me but they were of course all very welcoming. Cups of tea all round. I took my coat off and sat there. I had arrived, it felt like such an accomplishment. I didn't do anything; I just sat chatting to my colleagues, my friends, for a while and then drove home. I did this for the next few days before I was ready to turn on the pc and open my emails. But still I don't think I did any proper work. I would flick through files, read emails trying to take the information in but my mind only thinking of Abigail. There wasn't room for anything else. I certainly wasn't ready to meet any of my clients. I was still a mess, an absolute blubbering wreck, but I drove to work every day. In all honesty I probably shouldn't have gone back to work then, it was far too soon for me. But I needed to do something, I needed to at least try to focus on something else, even though that 'something' was actually impossible.

I think I was into the second week when I decided it was time to go and meet some of the providers and agencies that I worked with. I started to make arrangements to meet with people. My time-keeping wasn't very good as I would often have to pull over in my car to cry before I could arrive at my destination. I remember my manager telling me that my eyes don't have windscreen wipers. Everyone always seemed pleased to see me, surprised I was at work but pleased. This is the great thing about living in a very small community. I was slowly getting back into facing people, which was tough in its own right. If I had a pound for every hug I received I'm sure I would be a billionaire.

I really struggled to focus, to keep my brain engaged long enough on any task in hand. While reading emails my mind would wander, the tears would run, my heart aching for my daughter. I can't hide my pain away, my face shows exactly how I'm feeling, the tears are of course a huge giveaway too. But gradually I began to do more and more each day. I think it was a very long time before I can honestly say I was back in full swing.

Christmas parties were tough, everyone celebrating while inside I'm being torn to shreds. Missing my family, being away from them at Christmas time, staying away from home overnight was not what I wanted to do.

But company policy was that it was compulsory to attend the two away days each year. So reluctantly I went to the Christmas away day. Thanks to Matt who I danced with all night while the tears ran down my face. I struggled more than you could possibly imagine. Christmas songs I remember with my family, decorating the Christmas tree, parties we had been to. Abigail's favourite songs and those with tough words like "Spirit in the Sky" was so not what I wanted to hear. I felt like I was being tortured. My emotions were at an all time high as they always are at Christmas now. My colleagues Miranda, Steph and I were all sharing a lodge. Late that evening we all returned and sat chatting for hours. It's supposed to be a fun time of year for everyone and here they were stuck with me listening to all my stuff, feeling my pain with me. Eventually we all went to our rooms but only a matter of hours later I woke sobbing. Miranda heard me and came into my room. She held me tight in her arms while I cried like a baby. Life felt like hell and I just wanted to die.

The summer away day was always in May during Abigail's birthday. It couldn't have been any harder. My close colleagues could see how difficult this was but still it was compulsory. I had to send long emails explaining why I didn't want to attend before finally it was agreed by the directors that I could take the day off unpaid. They had no idea or understanding of what I had to go through just to write down why I didn't want to go. I had to relive all my pain.

* * *

I had been back at work over a year when I attended a conference in Inverness. During lunch we were seated about ten to a table with people from different organisations. My operations manager and colleague were with me and I knew some others from organisations that I worked very closely with. Of course in these situations people start chatting and you get asked who you work for and where you are based etc. When I answered 'I work in Wick, Caithness' a gentleman across the table from me said,

'Oh I've been there, it's a lovely place. I remember there were lots of people on the beach writing a message for someone. I think they died but I'm not sure who it was or what happened. I thought it was really nice though.'

Gobsmacked, I just sat there. He looked at me and said 'Do you know what it was for?'

'Yes,' I replied.

He just looked at me waiting for me to continue. I looked across to my colleagues feeling the pain well up inside me. My heart aching. I took a deep breath.

'I wrote it,' I continued, 'the message was for my daughter.'

'Oh,' he said 'what happened?' completely oblivious to all the emotions whirling up inside me.

I calmly explained my daughter had been killed in a car accident, while my thoughts were screaming please stop, someone get me out of here. I wanted the conversation to change, anything but this. But it didn't. He continued to ask questions and I struggled on, he then went on to talk about a tragic event in his life when he was younger. I really couldn't cope, I didn't want to hear it. In my head I was begging for someone to help me.

The fire alarm began to ring very loudly; we all just looked at each other. I whispered to my colleague next to me 'Saved by the bell' and managed a slight smile. We left the building and I burst into tears. Releasing all the emotion and pain I had been holding together in there. I didn't return. I drove back to the office in Inverness with my manager's permission and felt I had escaped.

There have been many occasions where I seem to end up in similar circumstances. I just wish the ground would open up and swallow me at times.

'It can't be easy for the people around you

to watch your pain every day'

Storm before the Rainbow

With every day that passes, I am one day further from the last time I saw Abigail. I miss her so much. The deep wrenching pain in my heart gets stronger every day.

But, with every day I know I am one day closer to the day I will die and I will be with her again. I long for this day.

No one can really describe the true, immense pain of grieving for a child; it goes too deep, your own personal black hole. No one can ever really understand. The closest to understanding are those that are living this too and we all grieve in our own way. We go through the grieving stages at different times.

Can anyone tell me how to feel or what to do? No. People try and often get it wrong. I know they're trying to help and be supportive. I'm extremely grateful for this even though I may not feel it at the time.

I'm not aware of anyone crossing the road to avoid speaking to me. Probably because like my friend Clare once told me, they would be more scared that I would cross the road and approach them. Which I probably would have done. I appreciate it must be very difficult to know what to say, I have been in the same situation myself, but saying nothing is worse. To be perfectly honest a hug says so much more than words can ever really say and I know of course this isn't always appropriate but it always lifts my spirits and helps to make me feel that little bit better than I did before.

The raw pain I feel in my heart will never leave and why would I want it to? For me, that would mean what happened to Abigail is Ok. It will never be Ok. Abigail is so very precious to us all.

I love her and I miss her. The pain is sheer agony; a stab through my heart. I want it to go away. I want my life to end. I want to be with Abigail. I want to hold her one more time. To kiss her, to hug her and to tell her that I love her. I want her back. I want her to come home. To walk back through that door and be with us once more.

Within the first few days of Abigail's passing I said I could feel a big black cloud heading my way. I knew I would need help and that anti-depressants wouldn't help me. They didn't when I gave up smoking years earlier; they blocked everything out and made me feel ill. St. John's Wort, a natural, mild anti-depressant, took the edge off things. It's all a bit like a rectangular coffee table with sharp edges. When I take anti-depressants the coffee table becomes invisible, it's still there but you can't see it. With St. John's Wort the coffee table is still there but at least its edges are softened to become oval and hurt less when you bump into them.

I know that St. John's Wort is a natural remedy and I read lots about it. I sought medical advice first and got my doctor's approval. So, knowing how it helps me I bought some ready for when the day came that I needed it. I knew I would. Six weeks after the accident I could feel my storm coming and so I opened the bottle knowing I would be taking this for a year. I wrote the date on the bottle and gave myself six months on it and six months to wean off, but it took much longer than that and sometimes I still need to go back on it for a few weeks or months to take the edge off things for a while again.

Just over a year later my storm was at its worst, the hurricane had finally arrived. How long it was here or how bad it would get, I just didn't know. I dealt with it day by day until it finally passed, but as I said, like all storms from time to time it returns.

In the early days during the sleepless nights and while still in shock I wanted to swim out to sea as far as I could so that I wouldn't have the energy to come back. I often thought of getting up and going while Paul and Hannah were asleep. The pain was just too much to endure sometimes. I felt I couldn't cope, couldn't go through this anymore and sometimes I still can't.

During the day I would drive to work, tears running down my face. They just wouldn't stop. Not really what you'd call crying, more a constant stream. I would think about driving off the road and crashing into a field, to end my life there and then, but I didn't. I don't know what kept me on the road. Close friends who I told how I was really feeling would often say to me 'But you have Paul and Hannah to think of. They both need you.'

To be perfectly honest, when you are in this dark and scary place, there is no one there but you. There's no room to think of anyone else. Somehow I need to stay here in this life for me, I need to carry on with my journey in my way. So, I'm not going to take my life, that's not for me, but I can understand those that do. I put one foot in front of the other and keep on going. Sometimes I feel I need my wellie boots on to get through the thick squelchy mud of daily life and other times I can skip along barefoot. As long as I keep putting one foot in front of the other I can keep up the momentum of life, no matter how slow it feels.

The thing to remember is I'm not suicidal, I'm grieving. But through grieving I feel suicidal. Now when I feel like this I ask myself the question that I have learnt while training to become a Samaritan in Cyprus, 'Do I want to die just for today or for the rest of my life?' and that's when I realise and say to myself through the uncontrollable sobbing 'Just for today.' I want to die today, for this to be my last on earth. But knowing it's just for the day the enormity of the intense pain begins to lift. It's only a matter of hours, less than one day before I know it will be gone. It doesn't seem so daunting then and somehow I manage to struggle through. The pain in my heart slowly lessens as the day goes on and I feel pleased that the day is nearly over. A better day will come tomorrow. I know this from experience now.

There were so many things I wanted to do with my life before Abigail's passing. I still want to do them; I just don't know what they are anymore.

The Storm

There is a thick dark storm looming
Dense black clouds are rolling near
It's frightening to see it coming
Not sure what to expect

I can see it in the distance
Coming closer and closer
Nowhere to hide, nowhere to run
All I can do is watch and wait

I sit with friends in glorious sunshine
Chatting, smiling, laughing away
Enjoying our day
But they can't see the storm nearby

While everything and everyone
Gets on with normal chores and
As the wind blows through the trees
I dread what's coming this way

I leave, get in my car and turn the key
Feeling sad, the loneliness appears
My face droops, tears begin to flow
No more strength to hide my pain away

The storm is getting closer now
Inside I scream for help
Alone with thoughts and feelings
No one here but me

The storm is huge
Lightning breaks
The thunder claps
I'm terrified what damage
The storm might bring

Depression is a scary thing.

Counselling

I used to wake up thinking I need help to deal with this, professional help. Someone I could scream and shout with, somebody who could take it all without being judgmental. I knew from the very beginning of my journey of grief that I couldn't do this alone.

I told my friends the day after Abigail's passing that I would need counselling to get through this.

Weeks and months passed and still I couldn't find help. Looking back I can see that I was looking in all the wrong places. I asked my doctor who suggested someone locally but they didn't feel right for me, too close to home.

I had heard about different bereavement charities but unfortunately they were not in our area and I would need to wait six months before some would see me anyway. I didn't really know how to go about finding anyone to help me. I felt desperate.

I spoke with Ruth our family liaison officer a few months later and explained to her that I was really struggling and needed counselling. I desperately wanted someone to help me through this. I had been told of a gentleman called John who was a counsellor and minister in Caithness but I had no idea how to get in touch with him. She said she would look into it for me. It felt like only minutes had passed when she called me back to say she had spoken to him and he was happy to meet with me. She had found his number in the phone book. I never even thought to look there! I needed to be referred by my doctor's surgery and so I made an appointment the next day.

I was referred and spoke to John; we arranged to meet at the chapel in Caithness General Hospital. He was a minister at a church in Lybster and was the hospital chaplain too. John was a very tall gentleman who spoke very quietly and calmly and was also very kind-natured and understanding. I warmed to him instantly.

He asked me what I thought counselling involved and if I was expecting answers.

'No,' was my reply, 'I need someone who I can scream and shout at who doesn't know me or Abigail. I just need to let it all out. I need help.'

John smiled and said that was fine, I could do it all.

He explained how he became a counselor and told me that if he saw me outside of our meetings in the street or say the supermarket he would walk past me as if he didn't know me. But John went on to explain that if he did people would likely know that I was meeting him for counselling.

'Oh that doesn't bother me,' I replied. 'I'll always say hello. I don't care if people know. I need help, what do they expect?'

I felt very rude but I needed to explain to John that I wasn't religious in any way shape or form. I don't fit in a pigeon hole of any specific belief. I believe in lots of bits of many religions but don't know enough about any to choose one in particular. I am more spiritual and think maybe we all believe in the same thing. I didn't want to offend him with any of my weird stuff and didn't want religion rammed down my throat. I couldn't understand that if there was a God why on earth would he take my beautiful daughter.

John smiled and nodded, yes he was a minister but he wasn't there to preach to me. I really liked him. And so my counselling sessions began. I don't think I ever screamed or shouted but it was nice to know he was there and if I wanted to, I could. I talked and talked and talked, which if you know me, you know that I do this a lot. It's shutting me up that's the problem. Many tears and tissues later I slowly began to feel better. There was a huge release of all the things I felt I couldn't say to friends and family yet. The true pain inside. John sat and listened. I knew he wasn't there to give me answers. I would find the answers myself and so I did. I had found my coping mechanism. It's amazing when you hear out loud your own thoughts and feelings how ludicrous some of them sound. It becomes easier to rationalise what's going on inside your own head and let out the emotions. An hour and a half later I would walk out the door happier and feeling that I could carry on with my life that little bit easier today.

John offered to help Paul and Hannah too if they wanted it. Paul didn't but I encouraged Hannah to come along to meet John so she could decide for herself.

Hannah would talk to John about her friends and what she had been up to at school. After a few weeks Hannah said 'I don't want to go anymore, I don't want to talk about it.'

I told her, 'That's Ok, you don't have to, we just needed to go and see if it would help.'

But the good thing was Hannah talked to me each week for the half hour drive there and the same going home. We had found a place to talk. Hannah could look out of the window and talk without having eye contact with me. We could sing to the radio in between and come back to talking. We just touched the surface, nothing too deep and emotional. I feel it really helped us both. We sometimes still use this method. Difficult subjects are always tough with teenagers but we have a solution that works for us. We get in the car and go for a long drive. Hannah laughs when I say, 'It's Ok, look out the window and talk out there, just make sure you're loud enough so I can hear you,' and then she would talk. Slowly but surely, difficult subjects become not so difficult after all.

Hannah attended "A day to remember" with the Crocus Child Bereavement Group in Inverness. Hannah really benefited from this day and went on a weekend camp with them as well which she thoroughly enjoyed. Hannah never really talked afterwards about what happened at the camp or what was discussed but she said she enjoyed it, which was the main thing for Paul and I.

My friends often say to me how lovely it is that Hannah tells me so much of what is going on in her life. Sometimes I have to say though it's like pulling teeth. My girls were always fairly open with me but obviously they kept things from me too. They're teenagers after all and you don't tell your Mum everything!

I met with John each week and then slowly our sessions naturally became less frequent. There wasn't a limit to the number of sessions I could have. John was there for as long as I needed.

I told him one day about my feelings when Abigail died, the things I was sensing. Weird stuff. I knew how she felt when she died, standing there looking at herself, her body, wondering what had happened to her. With her body unable to survive the accident, she couldn't come home so she went into the spirit world. I can recall sensing a young man being with her, helping her through her transition to the other side, helping her to understand where she was. John found comfort in my story as he thought this could be Jesus. He told me things from the Bible that could easily relate to this but I felt it was my cousin Alan who had passed in his early twenties, which I still believe was the case.

John and I would have some really interesting discussions about religion which I'm sure I usually started. He never pushed his beliefs on me. It was fascinating how similar our views and opinions were, we just had different names for the same explanations. John once told me that he thought I would find being inside the church very powerful and I often do. I sense an overwhelming amount of positive energy inside churches. It's a beautiful feeling, it's just the words that don't connect with me. Sorry, but they don't. Whenever I go inside a church I light a candle for Abigail. Her funeral service was in a church, so I guess I must believe in something because it always feels right but I never go to Sunday service.

I enjoyed my sessions with John and always left feeling more positive, a small amount of the weight on my shoulders lifted each time. We discussed Scott the driver of the car, my thoughts, feelings and views of the justice service and how he must be feeling. I said to John that I think one day I would want to meet him, to hear from him what happened that night but I wasn't sure if I would be able to cope and not sure if I would try to kill him or collapse in a heap. John told me I would know when I was ready and said that having got to know me and the kind of person I am I'd probably end up giving him a hug. I remember thinking 'never.' I hate him for what he's done.

'Talking about how you really feel can help to heal'

The Media

I understood the accident had to be reported in the local paper, but I hadn't expected it to be front page news. I didn't read it, it was all far too raw for me. I just wanted to buy it to keep in case one day in the future I might want to. Years on and I still haven't. It and all the other newspapers are safely tucked away in a box.

Some reporters unfortunately manage to get their facts wrong or misinterpret information. For instance, a reporter from a local newspaper interviewed Hazel who was in the car on that fatal night. They misunderstood what she said and reported that everyone was to attend Abigail's funeral with their faces painted orange! ORANGE?

The mother of one of Abigail's friends had called me the previous day on the reporter's behalf asking if we would give a televised interview for STV News which I had said 'No,' to. I was so angry that she had called us in the first place, but now I was fuming, steam coming out of my ears. I was supposed to be grieving for my daughter, yet instead I was angry with a reporter. An insensitive person, who had misunderstood when Hazel had said that she was wearing her make-up orange like Abigail. She, like most teenagers wore her make-up thicker. Make-up not face paint! I felt they only needed to think to realise this. So, I was then replying to texts and phone calls to say 'NO' to the orange face paint and had to explain to everyone. I really didn't need this. The consequences of their actions were catastrophic for my family and I.

I called Abigail's friend's mum and let rip, I went mad. I shouted that I wanted the reporter to stand outside the church and if anyone turned up with orange face paint on then they should be the one to ask them to leave and explain why. My daughter's funeral was not a circus!

They did write a nicer story a few days later. But still not the same as getting it right first time. I really didn't want to read everything that was printed just so that I was ready to explain if they or others got it wrong. It was a shambles.

Journalists as we know can be insensitive but was Hannah snuggling into her huge teddy at her sister's funeral really news? No, I don't think so. That's personal, that's Hannah's grief. The reporters were not welcome to attend the funeral, but they did. They weren't there to grieve for her or to pass on their condolences, they were there to write about it and earn a living, but this was our life. Apparently they sat upstairs out of the way. I don't care. They were not welcome and we didn't want to be front page news all over again. What I read was lovely but still an invasion of our privacy I felt. I suppose I should be grateful that they didn't come to the cemetery and take photos or film it. I may have been grieving and upset but I would have been extremely angry at that.

I can't believe they also charged us for Abigail's obituary when they used the information in their article on the front page!

* * *

Four and a half years on and I have finally spoken to the journalist who reported that everyone was going to Abigail's funeral with their faces orange. I told them exactly what I thought. I've held this anger inside me for such a long time, even speaking to them I was shaking and my heart pounding. I was still angry. But at least I got it off my chest and received an apology and I feel much better now, at last I can let it go.

* * *

I remember returning to work after the Christmas break, our first Christmas without Abigail. The worst Christmas of my life.

It was tough for those around me to talk about their celebrations as they knew this was difficult for me. It would be for anyone. I sat at my desk only to find the back page of the local newspaper sitting there with a huge photograph of Scott. The driver of the car on full view, not the smallest of pictures. I was horrified. Shocked.

I read the story about him scoring a goal. I can't remember the details, just the sense of feeling numb. The raging anger bubbling away inside me, they knew what Scott had done just a few months earlier. How could they print this and at this time of year? It was like nothing had happened. Yes life goes on, but to throw this in our faces infuriated me.

I called the newspaper and let rip. Shouting, how dare they, didn't they realise who Scott was, how insensitive could they be? Abigail was front page news for them for several weeks.

I couldn't believe the response I got. It was unimaginable. I felt they were showing that Scott was getting on with his life and would have had a great Christmas while mine was the worst there could possibly be, my family all having to live without Abigail and here they were rubbing our noses in it.

In my outrage I told the person on the phone to go with the reporter and the photographer to stand at the foot of Abigail's grave in Thurso and then go and write something nice about the bastard who put her there then. My hands trembling with anger, I could barely hold the phone. I slammed it down, not waiting for a reply. I sat at my desk sobbing in a state of total disbelief. My colleague looked at me in shock and passed me a box of tissues. Coreen and Helen as always came to the rescue with desperately needed hugs.

The response within the local community was the same as mine. A feeling of disbelief that the paper could be so insensitive. People, strangers even, approached me in the street to tell me what they thought.

It just seemed a completely thoughtless act, especially so soon after the accident. Now, nearly five years on, printing something about Scott scoring a goal, yes I can understand, but within a matter of months, no not at all.

* * *

The accident, my message on the beach and her funeral were all front page news and then again when the court case was heard twenty months later. Looking back I appreciate that no one actually came to our home, knocking on our door or camera crews sitting outside. We had been warned that this could happen and I am grateful that they didn't. STV news reported everyday at the time of the accident and the court case. From what little I saw I felt they were sensitive and am thankful for this and the lovely flowers that they sent us.

Nicola McAlley a reporter for STV News in Inverness always came across as very kind and considerate whenever I saw her in the High Court. She never approached us directly in the corridor or outside the building. I remember leaving the court room with Paul to walk back to the room set aside for us with Victim Support. Nicola was hurrying, I assume to meet her team to report on the news. She stopped in her track as we approached, bowed her head and waited as we passed. The respect she showed us in that moment touched my heart.

Nicola and a freelance reporter were both very caring when I read my statement for the news at the end of the hearing. For this I am so grateful. When giving my statement the reporter asked if he could use his Dictaphone, which I didn't mind. The camera and sound equipment were not in my face. They could see I was extremely nervous and were all very patient with me. Nicola calmly told me to take my time. She asked if I could answer a few questions afterwards and when I shook my head to say no, she didn't press me any further. Instead they thanked me. I remember the look on their faces, this wasn't easy for any of us. I really liked them both for their sensitivity.

The John O'Groat Journal was very supportive of my road safety campaign in memory of Abigail for her eighteenth birthday in 2010. I worked with a local journalist along with the Chief Inspector of Police and succeeded in giving a full story with advice on road safety.

In trying to raise awareness of this book I have been in contact with many journalists from television, radio, magazines as well as local and national newspapers. I have to say the support I have received has been incredible. All have been very kind, caring and understanding and so far I'm very pleased with the features and news reports that have helped me get the publicity I need.

So, as in all walks of life, you meet some people who are lovely and some who don't understand and are a little inconsiderate. I'm pleased I've met and spoken with quite a few of the kind and caring journalists.

'Spread the word and raise awareness'

Friendly Advice

Sitting at home one evening there came a knock at the door. To my surprise it was Jay and Alison, friends of ours who lived hundreds of miles away in Aberdeen. They had come back to Caithness to visit family and just popped round on the off chance we would be home.

Delighted to see them I welcomed them in. We sat in the kitchen chatting away for hours, catching up and reminiscing over old times. We all used to work together years earlier when Paul and I first moved to Caithness.

Jay made us laugh. They had originally knocked on the wrong door; someone had told them who we lived next door to but they assumed the house on the other side. No-one in. They went to get in their car to leave but as they got to our house they realised that our number plate wasn't fitting for the year of our car and realised it was our girls' names. Surely no coincidence they thought. I'd bought a personalised plate after Abigail died - AB52 HAN - Abigail and Hannah with the number two for my two daughters.

Jay and Alison sat and listened to us talk about what had happened to Abigail and what we were going through. I talked about feeling suicidal and this was the first time that Paul had heard me say this. I could see by the look on his face he was hurting, listening to the pain I was suffering inside, knowing that he couldn't help, no-one could.

Jay explained to us that he had come to check on Hannah more than Paul and I. I hadn't realised that his brother had died in similar tragic circumstances to Abigail. He understands what it's like to live without a sibling and after seeing what his parents went through he didn't want us to go down the same path. I think we helped each other that evening. For him to see a glimpse of what his parents were going through and we could understand a little of how Hannah must be feeling. He didn't want us to wrap her up in cotton wool and become over protective but he didn't want us to loosen the reigns and let her go off the rails. I will always be grateful for his advice. Often now when talking to Hannah, Jay's advice comes into play. I try to stay level-headed and think of Hannah as "Hannah" and not all the "what if's" that might happen to her. Hannah needs to live her life and not in her sister's footsteps. I think Paul and I are doing alright!

'Advice given freely is very seldom taken,

but listen anyway'

Panic Attacks

Unless you have ever suffered a panic attack you will find it very difficult to comprehend just how scary they are.

My first was only four months after Abigail's passing. I'd gone out for my friend Katrina's birthday. We went to the Holborn Hotel in Thurso for a meal and a few drinks on a dry but cold February evening. Having enjoyed my meal and spending time with friends I went to the bar to get a round of drinks. The bar wasn't busy that evening and one young lad was sitting there alone. I didn't know him but was aware that he was red-headed, slim and about the same age as Scott the driver of the car. I had no idea whether or not this was Scott but as the thoughts kept creeping into my head, I began to panic.

At first my chest felt tight, my lungs crushed, my heart aching, the pain was excruciating. I struggled to breathe, wheezing, unable to take a full breath, panicking for air but my lungs so tight there wasn't room to get the air in that I needed. I felt light headed and dizzy while at the same time having a pounding headache. My knees weak, barely able to breathe, I collapsed to the ground, terrified that I was going to die. Yet while all this was going on in my body, I was aware that the young man sitting at the bar may have been the person that killed my daughter. To say it was a terrifying experience is an understatement.

I was out of sight from my friends but luckily one of them had come to help me carry the drinks and saw me in a heap struggling to breathe. Not sure what on earth was going on she thought I was having an asthma attack and calmly helped me to breathe again. It seemed like an eternity had passed and when I felt like I had finally come to, the physical aching pain was so heavy, I was exhausted. The young lad in the meantime had already left. Eventually I managed to ask if he was Scott. The lady behind the bar said 'I don't know who he is, but he's not Scott.'

I felt stupid and awful that I may have terrified the poor young guy who had left and all for nothing. But at least I knew how I was going to react if I ever saw Scott. Not angry and wanting to kill him as I had thought but collapsing in a heap unable to breathe.

* * *

My second major panic attack was while out for lunch with my friend Debbie at the Pavilion restaurant near Thurso beach. We had been there for a while catching up on all our latest news when I noticed a young man with his girlfriend walk in. They stood chatting to the couple at the table next to us. He looked like Tyrone the driver of the other car on the night of the accident. But it wasn't anger that raged inside me at that moment, it was panic and dread.

At first I couldn't focus. I couldn't hear Debbie talking to me, it was like my body had been taken over, then I realised I wasn't breathing. Terror set in, then the same again, wheezing, struggling to get the air in; feeling like a giant was crushing my ribs together and squashing my lungs. Debbie wondered what on earth was happening and a lady at the next table called out to get me an ambulance as she thought I was having a heart attack. This made me panic further as I knew I didn't need an ambulance but all I could do was shake my head and try to speak. Debbie noticed this and said not to call for an ambulance. I knew I would feel a twit but I couldn't control what was happening to me. Then I broke down, my head collapsed over the table and I sobbed uncontrollably, but at least I could breathe again. Eventually, I managed to get Debbie to ask him to leave. I had slobbered all over the table, I felt so embarrassed I wanted the ground to open up and swallow me. Everyone was looking at me and I felt I couldn't even walk; my legs shaking.

The staff were very kind and allowed me to leave through the kitchen as he was still standing at the front door waiting to return. I asked Debbie if she could speak to him and ask if he was Tyrone, because if it was at least I knew who he was and if he wasn't I asked if she could apologise for me please. I felt like such an idiot, I didn't even know if this was him.

Debbie met me sitting on the promenade along from the restaurant, exhausted and drained by the whole experience. She had been speaking to him for a while. She said he was very understanding. It wasn't Tyrone but he knew that he looked like him and knew who I was. I felt sick inside and ashamed of how I had reacted, but I felt I had no control. I went home and slept for hours. I wanted these panic attacks to stop.

***

The severity of each attack varied but nonetheless all of them were utterly terrifying. Sometimes I could feel them coming on. Aware of the symptoms starting I would try to focus on my breath and stay calm, blocking out whatever was going on in my head, trying to control my emotions. Often easier said than done but I grew more successful each time. The fact I have learnt to meditate and focus on my breath has probably helped a great deal. I can't remember my last panic attack; it has been so long, thank goodness.

'Staying in control isn't without effort'

Abigail's Rainbow

I have seen a remarkable number of amazing rainbows over the last few years, but mostly in the first year after Abigail's passing.

It will always be incredible to see a rainbow and know when it's from Abigail.

The most astonishing day was when I travelled from my home in Scrabster to Bonar Bridge, about eighty miles away to meet a client for work. It started as a crap day, the tears just pouring and pouring, but as I got in my car that morning I saw a rainbow and I instantly knew it was a sign from Abigail and smiled.

As I started my journey I noticed another rainbow in the distance, the tears ran, I couldn't stop them. It was the longest journey ever. I had to pull over to cry and catch my tears, there was no apparent reason for the way I felt apart from the obvious; I was grieving. There were no triggers, all the songs that played on the CD seemed sad and brought back memories but I just continued with my journey. Every corner I turned there was another rainbow, one after the other and if I didn't see it in front of me or to the side, I could see it in my rear view mirror. It was unbelievable, so uplifting. The journey took me more than three hours with all the stops yet I had seen rainbow after rainbow, one always in my view for the entire journey. I felt amazing, uplifted and somehow able to get through the day.

What seems short of a miracle is that when I left my meeting later that afternoon I continued to see a constant array of rainbows the whole journey home too.

I feel so lucky to have received such a special gift from my daughter. You may think it all just a coincidence but inside my heart I know they were from Abigail.

When I arrived home from work Paul told me that he had seen an amazing rainbow that day at work which made him think of Abigail. My Mum called later that evening to tell me the same thing, they couldn't believe my story.

There have been so many occasions like this. Not just one, but several, one after the other, not always complete rainbows but just a section in the sky. I get great comfort from these events and feel so grateful.

* * *

I remember Paul driving Hannah and I home from Inverness one day when staring at the sky, it looked remarkable. The whole sky was pink, the clouds looked beautiful. As we approached the Berriedale Braes we saw a pink rainbow, yes a completely pink rainbow. Paul pulled over and we all got out and watched in amazement. There was not a single drop of rain in sight and yet here we were stood under this stunning pink rainbow in the midst of a pink sky that went on for miles. For us it had to be sent by Abigail.

Another favourite rainbow was on Abigail's birthday. Not long after feeling disappointed that I hadn't seen a rainbow, Paul returned home and told to me to quickly go to Abigail's bedroom and look out of the window. There I saw just a glimpse of one high in the sky. I smiled to myself and thought "Thank you Abigail." It couldn't be seen from any other room in the house. It was just what I needed.

* * *

My friend Max sent me an email with the cover of this book that he had designed for me. Paul and Hannah were at my house when I opened it. We were silent. I looked up at Paul who was standing over me, a tear in his eye, the same as me. It was beautiful, perfect. Paul and Hannah had to leave for her dancing lesson. Half an hour later Paul called me to say he had just seen a huge complete rainbow across the sky at Paphos. He said 'That's approval from Abigail for the cover of your book.' A few days later a friend had posted a picture of a Rainbow across Paphos on the internet for me, She'd been thinking of me. I'm not sure if it was the same rainbow that Paul had seen but the timing fitted. It was comforting to see and made me smile.

I get great comfort from these experiences yet they seem so few and far between now. But when I'm feeling really low, sure enough I am likely to see a rainbow in one form or another.

'Rainbows are the beautiful colours of life'

Abigail's bedroom, not a shrine

I would stand in the doorway of Abigail's bedroom, lean my head against the door frame. I would imagine in my head that she was at school, that she would be home soon. It took the pain away just that little bit sometimes.

Reality would kick in and the tears would roll down my cheeks until they fell off my chin and onto the carpet. No energy to wipe them. My heart aching.

I'd walk over to her bed, sit down and snuggle into her cushions and her teddy. I would lay there sobbing for hours. Not wanting to let her go.

Eventually I would slide the mirrored doors to her wardrobe open and stare at her things. The little trinkets she had neatly put on her shelf. Her make up and perfume all lined up. I knelt down to see her magazines at the bottom of the cupboard, pick one up and sit on her bed reading it. Knowing Abigail had read this. I would put it back exactly where I had taken it from, slowly close the door and open the other side. I would look in her chest of drawers, the little things like me that she kept, little keepsakes she had saved. A card her Nanny Margaret, whom she'd never met, had made. I would go through her clothes and remember the shopping trips when we had bought them.

I didn't want her room to become a shrine but none of us were ready to sort through her things and pack them away.

I agreed with Hannah that we would start to use her toiletries, her makeup and perfume. Hannah started to wear some of Abigail's clothes. After they had been washed Hannah always put them back in Abigail's wardrobe.

I asked Hannah what she would like of Abigail's to keep to remember her by and suggested that she take as many things as she wanted and put them in her room, but she didn't want to. She wasn't ready. Eventually Hannah and I chose the things we wanted to keep for ourselves, things we wanted our family to have and things we could give away.

Slowly I started to work my way through Abigail's school stuff and bits and bobs her friends had given her as gifts for birthdays and Christmas. I couldn't keep all of this, what was I going to do with it? I decided to ask her friends if they would like the things they had bought, they have the added memory of buying it for her and when they gave it to her. These things meant more to them than they did to me. Hannah and I chose school books that we wanted to keep and gave the rest to her friends who had been in her class.

I put things together for my dad, my sisters and my nephews; little things like teddies, belts and books for them to remember her by. Hannah and I packed them all in boxes and put them in the post.

Slowly but surely things started to leave Abigail's room, not huge amounts at once, nothing too scary. It wasn't until we moved two years later before I completely cleared her room. I loved Abigail's bedroom and so did she.

'It's not easy to let things go'

Family and Friends

Why is it when we feel so low and desperately need the love and support of family around us we look around and believe that they're not there? They are living with their own grief, afraid of how you may react, unsure what to do, so sometimes they do nothing. This seems like the most harmful pain they could cause to you, to me. It's devastating. Your life has fallen apart and everything around you is so different; depression, immense sadness, no one knows or understands how you are suffering. The people you most want to talk to, to be with, you feel are not there for you. It takes so much courage to pick up that phone and ask for help. So when you try to call on many occasions and no one answers, its heart breaking, you can't leave a message. They don't even know you called.

Family always believe they know you best and the other extreme are those family members who say the most bizarre things and blurt out what they're thinking. Impose their beliefs on you or even worse tell you how you're coping and yet they think this is Ok to do. Screaming inside for them to be quiet, thinking please don't say anymore. Their beliefs and understanding are so different from mine.

Sometimes family members will speak to you on days when you feel like absolute crap and are desperate to say how you feel but they are busy telling you about their day and their life. They don't even realise you've been trying to speak but nothing coming out. The pain in your head and your heart is fire within, so desperate to be released, but there is no one there to listen, no one to help you let go, to let it all out. So you do much of it alone.

You know what though - I can look within myself and see that I too have done the same in so many different situations. I have been like all these family members. I thought I knew best, I thought not saying anything would help and sometimes, in fact often, I would say too much. Now I really understand that we have no idea what's going on inside each other's heads, behind closed doors, eyes wide shut, peace and pain together within.

It feels like it takes so much longer to deal with your emotions alone, it's so painful and raw. The depression within deepens and you find it difficult to let go. But along the journey somehow you do. It takes time and you appreciate the friends who are there for you, who listen and try to understand. They find it difficult to watch from the outside in. They are the ones who listen, who you can talk to, who you can really let go of all your pain with. They find it hard to understand why your family are not there for you but that's because friends often see the real me.

The honest truth is that no one can really help you or me, no one can do right for doing wrong. Sometimes I don't even understand what's going on inside my own head so how on earth can I expect anyone else to? People will ask 'How are you?' not 'How do you feel?' but the 'How are you?' comes with a tilt in the head and that look in their eye, you know what they mean. But today, I was coping and feeling great and now that question has just put me straight back to when I heard that Abigail had died and all the pain and emotions that come with that have come flooding back. Other times I may feel like crap, suicidal and really want someone to talk to. That's when I need someone to ask me how I feel but they don't. It's a lose, lose situation. If only sometimes our thoughts were written across our foreheads then nobody need ask anything and could just see that a hug is all I or you need. A hug so easily takes away the pain. It's like an instant release and no words or thoughts are needed.

It's your friends that you tell your true feelings to and let go of your emotions with. Your barriers collapse and your family don't see this. So of course your family see you as strong, think that you are coping and believe that you're alright. When really all you truly feel is that your world is falling apart and there is no one there to catch you. Afraid that by saying to your family how much you need them or how much pain they are causing you will bring an even bigger rift between you all. To be honest initially it does. But maybe, you can all understand and let go together? Who knows what the answer is? After all, we are all suffering and each of us needs to deal with this in our own way.

Eventually things do get better. My relationships with family members have all improved. We get on really well now. We can all laugh and joke together but when it comes to talking about Abigail, silences emerge. It's tough for all of us and I can accept this. It has been really difficult for me to write this chapter. I have struggled with it, starting over and over again, deleted and re-written, nothing really feels right. I don't want to hurt my family if and when they read this. But the purpose of this book is, I hope, to give understanding of what really goes on behind closed doors and what goes on inside my head! So if this chapter can help someone out there who is suffering too, then I hope that this makes sense and can bring comfort to know that really and truthfully there is no right or wrong.

Isn't it great though that we are all different? Life would be so boring if we were all robots! No-one's family is truly perfect, accept this. I know I'm not perfect; there are so many things I could have said or done differently. Looking back at the pain I was in, it seems impossible for me to have even thought about alternatives. No excuse, it's just my reason, we all have them. My advice, if you can't get the support you need, find a close friend who can help. Keep your family relationships and always know that you are suffering together silently. Send a loving hug through your thoughts out there in the universe for them to receive. I'm sure they're sending you one back.

'A hug can say a thousand words'

Difficult Situations

Hannah and I went to a Girl Guiding Gala Dinner, a fundraising event for the centenary celebrations. We went with my friend Katrina and her daughter Freya. The seating arrangements were pre-planned. We were sat at round tables that generally seated eight. There were seven on our table, the four of us and three visitors who had travelled from Edinburgh to attend. We all introduced ourselves. They were two sisters with one of their husbands, a quiet gentleman. I knew everyone else in the room as it was mostly people from Girl Guiding with their families. Many of my friends were there, people I knew, people I was comfortable with.

I often find it very difficult to meet new people as I'm always asked the difficult question that I just want to avoid; how many children do you have? Unfortunately this is one of those horrendous situations where strangers often can't stop asking more and more difficult questions even when I politely ask them to change the subject.

This time it was Hannah in the firing line. The lady closest to Hannah asked her if she had any brothers or sisters. A normal everyday question, but for us so difficult! Hannah replied 'No, I'm an only child,' and looked over at me. I was heartbroken. I tried my best to hold back the tears and a few minutes later excused myself to go to the bathroom. I walked calmly out of the hall and sat on the stairs crying. I couldn't stop, unable to bring myself together. I felt for Hannah. Katrina came and hugged me, knowing I was suffering.

When I finally sorted myself out, I got up, checked I looked as reasonably Ok as I possibly could and walked back to our table. I whispered to Hannah 'It's alright, I'm fine,' because I could see she was worried. It wasn't a problem what Hannah had said, it was the fact that she was in this situation and I couldn't protect her. I, on one occasion have said I only have one daughter as I felt this was easier than dealing with the questions afterwards and on tough days you really don't want to address this. I hated it and have never done it since.

The same lady then turned to me and asked 'So, why did you only have one child?'

Screaming inside I wanted to shout 'Will you just shut up!' but I ignored her, pretending I didn't hear, then turned to her sister sitting next to me and asked 'Could we change the subject please?'

She asked 'Why?'

I thought, oh for heaven's sake where did these people come from! I explained 'It's difficult for us.'

Again she asked 'Why?'

I wanted to get up and walk out, I turned to Katrina, she just stared in amazement at the whole situation. Then she too was asked why she only had one child. Katrina and I just chatted amongst ourselves trying to ignore them, when one of them asked again. There could be a number of reasons why people only have one child; choice, unable to have more, or my case, along with so many other reasons. All the same, it's none of their business and you would have thought they would have got the message by now, but sadly no.

I whispered to the lady next to me, 'My eldest daughter was killed in a car accident. This is very difficult for us, now please change the subject.'

'Oh what happened?' she asked. The questioning still continued.

I sat in silence and ignored her just wanting to leave. Our whole evening was completely ruined. There were so many supportive friends I wish we could have sat with. It was still very early days for us to cope with all of this.

There's no one word for parents who have children who have passed away. For husbands and wives there is widow and widower, one word which explains so easily without explanation. For parents like us we don't have anything. When asked 'How many children do you have?' I have a multiple of choices I can reply with. I can either say one not including Abigail, or say two and not explain further, which is where I usually end up being asked further difficult questions or my preferred choice is to just explain straightaway. It's tough, my chest goes tight every time and I need to focus on my breathing. It makes people feel uncomfortable, me included. It would be helpful at times to have one word that explains this. The only thing is that all of us parents out there who share this don't want to be labeled or in the same club but it would be so useful sometimes.

* * *

I hate calling call centre's at the best of times but on this occasion I needed to call the AA to amend my car insurance. Everything sorted within a matter of minutes, brilliant, but oh no, there had to be the additional sales attempt! 'Would you like to increase the value of your insurance in case of an accident?'

'No, thank you,' was my reply, ready to put the phone down.

But as is her job, the lady was persistent going on to tell me about the benefits in case someone died in an accident. My breath stopped.

There are no benefits. No amount of money can ever repay the life of someone, let alone my daughter.

In shock, the beginnings of a panic attack started. My breathing changed and she could obviously hear this. She asked, 'Are you Ok?'

I just about managed to spit out 'No,' then began uncontrollably sobbing. I struggled to speak. I probably should have just put the phone down but I was in shock and didn't think. In the end I managed to tell her about Abigail. The lady at the end of the phone began to cry. She was sorry. This wasn't her fault; she was only doing her job, but both our days were now ruined.

I ended the call, curled into a ball on the sofa and just let all my pain out, the howling seemed uncontrollable.

I felt an arm wrap round me, it was Hannah. She had heard me, walked downstairs and cuddled up next to me, looking after her Mum. I love her so much; we shouldn't have to go through this.

'If only people could understand'

Normal day to day stuff

It was a long time after the accident before it became habit to only get three plates out for dinner. Every night without thinking I would get four and as I put Abigail's back in the cupboard I would feel the sorrow inside, the emptiness, my face solemn, missing her. Wondering what she would have wanted for dinner that night? There was always too much food, I would split it three ways so that we shared her meal.

I would struggle to set the table for three, always wondering where Abigail would have sat. Our new dining table didn't arrive until after the accident. Paul, Hannah and I agreed not to have our own set place every day, so each day we would change seats and sit at different ends of the table just so that we didn't have a routine where Abigail was missing. Of course she was, but there wasn't a set place where she would have sat. Nothing was easy. In the end we often sat in the living room with our plate on our laps in front of the television, something that used to be a rarity in our house but became a common occurrence.

* * *

Normal chores often felt impossible to cope with. Cutting the grass was one of the most difficult. I think because it took so long to do it gave me too much time to be alone with my thoughts. We had a large garden and the repetition of walking up and down became monotonous, my mind would wander, my thoughts always of Abigail. I would stop, break down in tears unable to take another step. Paul would walk over to me and hug me, just holding me tight while I sobbed, letting out my pain. I'd wipe my tears, look at Paul and try to smile. Not a word spoken. I would start the lawnmower and continue cutting the grass, my thoughts never leaving me. It wasn't long before Paul would come and take over from me. He would mow a couple of strips. Leaving the garden a third maybe even half cut, he would put the mower and tools away, leave it till another day. He felt the same as me. Sometimes it would take us days before the grass was fully cut.

Paul and I met a lovely couple who were on holiday here in Cyprus in our complex only a week after we had moved here. They told us the story of a friend of theirs whose child was very sick. They wanted to help but felt there was nothing they could do. The parents spent all their time at the hospital. I suggested they could offer to help by doing normal chores for them. For some this may be an invasion but for others it could be an enormous help. It would have been for us.

* * *

In the days and weeks after the accident people would come into our home and take off their shoes before walking into our living room. I would look at them and say 'Don't worry you can leave them on.' But still everyone took them off. I would shrug my shoulders and think that was nice.

Often my friends would say 'You're in your new home and you would want us to take them off.'

After what happened to Abigail absolutely nothing else mattered. I really didn't care anymore. But they were right; I would have wanted them to take their shoes off before and am grateful that they still did.

* * *

I went to see Nelia my hairdresser about every five weeks. I couldn't face going for a while as I didn't want to be around other people all chatting in the salon about their day and lives, all the fun and excitement along with all the local gossip. So, Nelia very kindly used to cut my hair on a Monday afternoon when no one else was around. It was a while before I returned to normal routine and could cope with other people being there but one Monday afternoon Nelia had taken a booking for a hair colour that overlapped with my appointment which of course was fine.

I had started to notice more grey hair on one side of my head and was concerned. I asked Nelia to check my roots for me as I have always coloured my hair red. Nelia looked up into the mirror at me and I could see by her face that I was now grey. She told me it was Ok it was only one side of my head. I cried so much, the stress and shock had turned my hair grey within a matter of months.

The lady sitting near me said, 'It's alright, it happens to us all.'

Maybe so, but I was thirty four with the odd grey here and there and now all of sudden the whole right side of my head was grey. I was so angry with Scott for this too, not only had he done what he'd done to Abigail but now my hair too! My body was already in physical pain through grieving and now this, I was shattered to pieces.

* * *

I wanted to change so many things in my life. Run away and hide from the life I was living, to be someone else, somewhere else and leave everything behind. That's not reality though and I can safely say that no matter where you are in the world the pain and hurt inside never leaves. It travels with you. I was often advised not to do anything within the first year. That's when mistakes and regrets are strongest apparently. Too many changes can suddenly creep up and bite you when you turn to look for the comfort of the one we miss. I think the only thing I changed in our first year was our car. I loved our Seat Leon, so many happy memories of places we had travelled to. Remembering the funny journeys laughing and joking along the way and even the arguments, but mostly laughter. When I handed the keys over in the garage and collected my new car I felt sick. I drove off unhappy with my new car, feeling miserable inside. I was missing the old one already, my comfort zone with many memories left behind. There was nothing inside this car that had any reminder of Abigail. I had removed everything from the glove box of the Seat and put everything in the new car, a pair of Abigail's old glasses were there along with a small teddy. I had removed it from the charity bag where she had put her stuff the day before she died. The teddy now sits in my kitchen and her glasses are in the glove box of my current car. There is no harm in having them there, they don't make me sad anymore, they are part of my belongings, the things I have around me.

* * *

It was months later before I went into Skinandi's nightclub in Thurso with some of my friends. A birthday I think or someone's celebration. It took me ages to get ready, unlike me. I never usually took long to get ready to go out and enjoy myself. I can get ready in fifteen minutes if I have to. But this particular night it took forever.

Eventually Paul and I left the house and met our friends in the pub. Beginning to enjoy ourselves again, putting on a brave face. By midnight we were in Skinandi's having a few drinks. We were up dancing and enjoying ourselves when somebody I knew came over to me and whispered in my ear 'It's nice to see you out enjoying yourself.'

This floored me. Unbeknown to her she put me right back to the night Abigail died. My thoughts now unable to deal with enjoying myself anymore. My night ruined, I was destroyed. I found Paul and together we left. I crawled into bed, cuddled up to Paul and sobbed. I wasn't ready to have fun. She didn't mean any harm I know and it's nice that she was pleased I was enjoying myself. I just didn't need to hear it that night.

* * *

Just recently I went to a DIY store in Essex with my friend Nigel, he needed to buy some materials for the car he was rebuilding. As we walked through the shop I wandered into my own little dream world reminiscing when Paul, Abigail, Hannah and I used to go into the same store in Romford.

I told Nigel that Paul would be looking through the power tools section while Abigail and Hannah played in the Kitchens pretending it was their own home while I ran around the store collecting all the items we needed; decorators caulking, paint, plug sockets etc.

As we walked towards the lighting area I saw a lamp I knew Abigail would have loved. I paused for a moment considering buying it for Hannah. I felt solemn inside, missing my family life, the tears welled in my eyes. Nigel put his arm around me to comfort me. This is over four years on now and still there are tough times, there always will be. I never thought wandering around the store that day would stir up so many emotions. We left and got in his car, the tears streaming down my face, the pain within me, back to square one again. It hurts so much.

The problem is you know, in reality, every month is tough. Every day of every week there is something to remind me that Abigail should be here with us. Sometimes people say 'Oh it's difficult at certain times of the year.'

Yes they're right; Abigail's birthday, the anniversary of the accident and her funeral as well as Christmas are all the most difficult for me. I can feel these coming well ahead of time and I need to deal with the aftermath within me for months after too. So, you see these take up the whole year on their own.

But in truth every month has something. January it's the aftermath of Christmas and Paul's birthday. Celebrating our own birthdays without her is horrendous too. February; Valentine's day, we always did something as a family. It's Hannah's birthday in March along with Mother's Day and April is usually Easter. That's just the first four months of the year. The list goes on.

May is Abigail's birthday. June: Fathers Day. July and August; school holidays, Abigail will never have left school in my mind. September back to school, preparing for the new school year.

October half term holidays, Abigail died on the first day of the school holiday, each year the date is different. But for us we have the actual day the 6th October, then the first Saturday of the school holidays, then the anniversary of her funeral on the 16th October. End of October is our wedding anniversary where Abigail was our witness. I relive the wonderful memories of this day over and over in my head all day.

A week later, beginning of November is my birthday. I hate it. I try to enjoy my birthday but all I want is Abigail here. Then of course December and the preparation for another Christmas.

A whole year over, New Years eve, missing her, feeling sick, another year has passed. Another year having lived without her and here we are faced with another year to follow. We have to go through it all over again. Every day, every week, every month something to remind us that she's not here. I'll be honest; some of it never gets easier. I hate having to live without Abigail, I miss her terribly.

'Life goes on with or without us'

Saying Goodbye

Months on, I woke in tears in the middle of the night from a bad dream, feeling like I had just been in the car accident with Abigail. I can still recall it so vividly.

I was in the back of the car with her, I was sitting where Hazel had actually been, behind Scott. I felt the car hit the pillar at the end of the wall, spin and come to a stop. I jumped out of the car and saw that Abigail had too. She ran back towards her friends who were all standing there behind the car watching. Abigail ran to Becca, hugged and kissed her then went back and sat in the car where she had been.

I went to her, unsure what I was going to see. I bent down to touch her, to help, to look after her. I knew she was dying. I went to kiss her and she said, 'Don't touch me Mum my skin is all horrible.' We looked at each other in tears. She said 'Bye Mum' and peacefully closed her eyes and went.

I woke, my eyes filled with tears. Abigail had said goodbye. It was so real, as if I'd really just been there with her with all the emotion and pain of reliving the news all over again. Paul woke and hugged me, it was a usual occurrence for me to lie in bed crying, my pillow soaked in tears.

He would just lie and hold me in his arms to comfort me. Sometimes I would slowly drift back off to sleep. Other times I would just lie there still and silent while the tears ran, unable to sleep again with the thoughts running through my head all night, missing Abigail

'It's never easy to say goodbye, if we ever really do'

Holidays

Booking a holiday would seem like a simple task, something to be excited about. Talking about it and planning is relatively easy. However, when I come to research and booking it's a whole other ball game. I go online and look through different travel agents websites - the destinations all look and sound wonderful, a break desperately needed from the everyday life we live. Time to get away.

I smile and feel I have found something to look forward to. I click on the dates we have chosen, select the destination, Salou in Spain on this occasion, and then here it comes two adults, one child....I break down, can't go any further and just stare at the screen. My eyes well up with tears, the emptiness appears. It takes days, sometimes weeks for me to build up the courage to start again. I have to do it one day. So here I go again, another attempt and the same thing happens all over again. Failure. It has taken years for this to get easier, but it doesn't go away. I pause when I get to this stage. Mentally I say two children, even though now she would be charged as an adult. But this is how I cope.

Now the holiday for the three of us is finally booked, we all get excited and start thinking about what we will do and start planning ahead. Shopping for clothes, sun cream etc. But seeing the things Abigail would choose in the shops is heartbreaking, missing her all the time. It's tough.

The day is approaching for us to leave - time to start packing. It's awful, horrendous. How can I possibly pack the suitcases without packing Abigail's clothes, the stuff she would need? She always took up more space than the three of us put together. I can't, I sit and sob, angry, stressed, shouting at Paul and Hannah. I can't take this anymore, I don't want to go.

Paul finishes the packing, I get out what I need and Paul does the rest. He's never forgotten anything. He's travelled plenty of times before so there really is no need for me to obsess, worry or stress.

We drive to the airport and begin to feel excited, thinking of all the things we are going to do.

As we board the plane my heart is pounding, time to go to our seats. Again a simple task it would seem. It says where we are sitting on our tickets. Nobody knows that we always sat two and two, usually Abigail and I and Paul with Hannah either in front or behind us. Not anymore, we sit in a line of three. I look at the seats behind, then I look in front. I don't want to be here, I want to sit with Abigail. I sit in silence, missing her. Missing her excitement, her laugh. I hear everyone bustling to get to their seat, putting their luggage in the overhead lockers, laughing, excited about their holiday. Paul looks at me and asks if I'm Ok. He can tell by my face that I'm not. He holds my hand and looks knowingly at me. We all miss Abigail. We try our best to continue with our lives but it will always be difficult.

Restaurants are the same. I really struggle when the three of us go out for a meal and we're asked, 'How many would you like a table for?' Easy question. We're directed to a table for four and the extra place setting is removed. My heart sinks, they're taking Abigail's place away. I stare at the empty chair. We try to carry on, but it's far from easy, even with the time that's passed I still feel the same. If I see a round table I usually ask for that one.

Holiday excursions can be wonderful but they can also be horrible at times, depending on the people you meet while you're there. Meeting strangers on holiday enjoying themselves having a great time can be difficult. Sometimes the best way to see things is on an excursion but when we really want to be left alone and enjoy our day it can be difficult. I'm often faced with people making polite conversation asking, 'Where are you from?' 'What do you do?' and then here it comes, 'How many children do you have?' Some people I feel comfortable with and explain while others I feel like saying 'Piss off and leave me alone,' but I don't. I try to change the conversation or leave, but I don't think I've said that to anyone yet and don't think I'm likely to either really. It's not their fault, it's a normal question, but for me I just can't cope with it sometimes.

We take so many things for granted. The rest of the holiday is much the same. We try to please each other and muster all the energy we can to look happy until it all erupts and we discover that all three of us are feeling the same. We all miss Abigail. We all want her to be here with us. The sun is shining, everyone around us is having a fabulous holiday and we all feel like crap, miserable. We sit together in tears of silence, we finally decide to go and do something else. We talk about what Abigail would have liked. What she would do. We can smile and laugh when we talk about her like this. We start to enjoy ourselves. We have brought Abigail into our holiday.

Arriving home, seeing friends, back at work, the first thing everyone says is, 'Did you have a nice time?'

'Yep, had a brilliant time, thank you,' is our reply and we retell all the happy parts. They don't want to hear the tough stuff.

* * *

We booked a farm house in Aviemore, in the Highlands of Scotland for October 2008 with our friends Julie and Pete and their four girls; Jay, Sian, Jodie and Sophie. We have been very close friends for many years. The girls were my bridesmaids with Abigail and Hannah and our niece Sophie. They now range from teenagers to adults in age.

We were all looking forward to our holiday, planning activities the girls would all like: places to go, things to see and do. They drove up from Essex and we travelled down from Caithness. We all met in Aviemore, so excited. The girls hadn't seen each other I think since Abigail's funeral, so it was nice to be together again.

The next day was our wedding anniversary, I was struggling to cope. I relived my whole wedding day in my mind, missing Abigail. Here were five of my bridesmaids all running around the house on holiday. Abigail should have been here with them, enjoying herself too. I tried to hold it together, disappearing to my room if I needed to cry. I didn't want to ruin anyone's holiday.

We went quad biking one day. We had so much fun yet inside I was utterly miserable, finding every moment more difficult than the last.

Landmark Forest Adventure Park was on everyone's list for our next day out, oh boy, it couldn't have been any tougher. I struggled to get out of bed that morning, my body riddled with grief and misery. I didn't say anything.

We arrived and all were busy looking at what attraction they were going on first. I just held onto Paul, he knew. I had arranged a day trip for the Brownies in Caithness and Abigail had come along with her friend Becca for the day too. Here I was surrounded by so many memories. The hardest for me was the Ropeworx. It's a high wire course in the treetops. I'm scared of heights and was terrified watching as Abigail went round and felt very proud of her when she completed it. I now stood under the Ropeworx wishing I was watching her again that day.

I wandered around, my face solemn. Everyone was trying to have fun but I think they all thought I was annoyed with them, but I wasn't. I would try to smile but my heart was so sad that I found it impossible. I was just struggling to cope and constantly in tears but I tried not to let them see. I was living in hell. I was snapping at the girls for no reason the whole time we were away. I climbed to the top of the water slide with Julie and suddenly burst into tears. She just held me tight while I sobbed. I cried out,

'I miss her Julie, I miss her so much. I want her to come home.'

'I know,' she said and just held me.

My knees were giving way below me, I felt sick. My pain won't leave me, it still hurts today remembering it all. It was all too much too soon for me. It was only a year on. Abigail's anniversary had just passed, it was our wedding anniversary and the following week, my birthday. It couldn't have been any more difficult really. I thought it would be nice as it might take my mind off it all, but no, it just heightened everything.

I felt like I ruined everyone's holiday. I stayed at their house recently and we were looking through the photos again. I began to cry as I recalled all those awful feelings back then.

I must have said 'I'm sorry,' a thousand times for ruining it.

They all have happy memories though and said it can't have been that bad, we're still friends.

'Nothing's ever easy'

A Bridesmaid at last

Yes, at last in my thirties, a bridesmaid! I was honoured when Maria called and asked me to be one of her four bridesmaids. I know, I know, Maid of Honour is the real title because I'm married and over the hill, but tough, I've never been a bridesmaid so to me that's what I was and loved it.

Maria didn't have anywhere to store her wedding dress away from Derek the groom to be. I offered Abigail's room, the perfect place, her room wasn't being used and it was something happy and positive going on in my life. I was delighted when she accepted, it made me smile every day to see Maria' dress in there.

Sometimes it was tough going through wedding plans with Maria, thinking to myself I will never get to do this with Abigail. It would have been so exciting to plan a wedding with her. Who knows what it would have been like? Over the top more than likely but stunning I'm sure. She had way out ideas sometimes but when it came to crunch time her ideas were always lovely. I only had to look at her elegant black and white bedroom that she had designed and loved for me to know this.

It was always difficult meeting new people back then, only a year on. The hen night was a blast, we went to Top Joes in Scrabster. We had the place all to ourselves and it was easy enough for me to meet Derek's family and other friends of Maria's while surrounded by so many friends. We had such a great time. Derek is a farmer so the fancy dress theme for the night was yep, farm animals. Maria was the milkmaid of course and the idea for us, the four bridesmaids, yes you've guessed it, cows! Not just any old cow but ones with enormous boobs with black bras! We looked stunning of course.

We later went into Thurso to the Comm Bar. Oh what a tit I felt now in my fancy dress outfit. I met up with Paul and our friend Colin. Colin made lots of funny comments and said how lovely my costume was and how he had always wanted to be a "Coo" (Scottish word for cow by the way!) So I offered to swap clothes. Colin was up for it so I began taking his jeans off, but couldn't get past his "Cat" boots, his jeans left hanging round his ankles. Kyla his girlfriend tried to help, while Paul just stood there laughing at us all. We all had such a giggle, it was a brilliant night with many happy memories that I will never forget. Colin has since passed away and Paul, Hannah and I miss him so much.

While out looking for a wedding present on Maria and Derek's list I bumped into some of the wedding guests who had been to the hen night. One lady recognised me and said,

'Oh, you're one of the bridesmaids aren't you, I can't remember your name, sorry.'

'Yes, I'm Nicky,' I smiled.

'Oh yes, it's the other one whose daughter was killed in the car accident wasn't it?' she said.

My face dropped, 'No that's me,' I replied, struggling to hold it together.

I made my excuses minutes later and left. I sat it my car and cried my eyes out. A mess yet again. Pull it together

Nicola I thought and drove off to the supermarket. I pulled into the car park, struggling but determined to be normal; like everyone else. I had only managed to walk round the first two aisles when I met my friend Diane. Thurso being a small town, you can't go anywhere without bumping into someone you know. I was so pleased to see her, a friendly face, but when she asked with her usual beaming smile, 'Hi, how are you?' I couldn't help but burst into tears. She hugged me while I sobbed uncontrollably.

'It's Ok, let it out,' she whispered to me, feeling the pain I was in.

Eventually she asked me what had happened.

'I want to be known as Nicky not that lady whose daughter was killed.'

I went on to explain.

I can't remember if I bought anything, I just went home and spent the afternoon on the sofa, a miserable wreck once again. I should have shares in tissue manufacturers.

When it came to the big day we were all so excited getting ready round at Maria's house, the five of us girls; real girlie time. We were ready and the cars arrived to collect us. I walked outside and saw the black limousine, 'Oh my God,' was the thought in my head. She had ordered the cars from Dunnett's who not only do funerals but also weddings along with many other things. My breathing changed, my chest grew tighter, here it comes, I could feel a panic attack coming on but determined not to ruin any part of Maria's day I pushed on and told myself it was Ok. I slowed my breathing and thought I was in control. We all got in the car, the girls laughing and giggling, singing silly songs and I suddenly became an absolute mess. I got out of the car and ran down the road. At first no one knew what on earth was going on; Kirsty suddenly realised and came after me.

'I can't get in that car, I can't, it's a funeral car and I know I never used it for Abigail but I just can't, I'm so sorry,' I blurted out.

The florist arrived we tried to work out a way of fitting me in their van to take me to the wedding. George from Dunnett's arrived in the Rover that we used for Abigail's funeral. Suddenly I was Ok. I could cope. George my saviour once again. He whispered to me, that it wasn't a problem; I could travel with him if I wanted. He knew I was alright with what I call Abigail's car but not the big black limousines. He apologised as he had only just heard that I was one of the bridesmaids. He knew I wouldn't be able to cope.

As a surprise for Maria this car wasn't for her as she thought, moments later a carriage with two shire horses came round the corner and along the road towards us. It was lovely to see Maria's face light up. They'd been brought over from the Orkney Isles as a gift for her from one of her friends. Off the girls went in the limo, while I sat in the front of the rover with George laughing away, while Maria followed in the horse and carriage.

After the service we drove to Sandside Estate for the photos, of course by now George, Maria and Derek all knew there was no way I could get in the Limo. So, I went in the front of the Rover with George again while Maria and Derek sat in the back. It was a giggle and I'm so glad they didn't mind.

Colin, one of Derek's two best men had a whisky flask in his sporran. He offered some to me. I kept sipping. He said it was Bacardi not whisky. It was lovely and just what I needed. By the time we were moving on to the waterfalls at Forss House Hotel for the next set of photos I was feeling more relaxed and agreed to sit in the limo while we waited for Maria and Derek. I couldn't close the door but I sat there with the help of all the bridesmaids, best men, ushers and Colin's hip flask of course. We were enjoying ourselves and being occupied was helping to keep my mind off where I was. When it came to leaving I had decided it was time to deal with my fear of this car. I agreed with the help of the others and a little more alcohol intake that I would travel with them and so I did. Fortunately it was a very short journey. Tough but I made it. The rest of the day went according to plan. What a brilliant time we all had.

'Facing fears can help to heal'

Anniversaries

After my message on the beach I had a huge bond with so many of Abigail's friends, some of whom I hadn't really met or got to know that well before. But now we all shared something so horrible - we all love and miss Abigail. Lost together with what to do about it.

The 6th October was approaching, her first anniversary. I had no idea how on earth I was going to cope. Stressed, angry, hurting inside, constantly upset, I wasn't coping at all. But I needed to do something.

Sinclair and Veronica came round for dinner on the actual date, with their lovely daughter Hannah. We had Indian takeaway, a curry, just like we had the previous year but this time I didn't cook. Sitting around the house really doesn't help me. I didn't want to sit there clock watching all night. I had already relived the day over and over again from the moment I woke that morning. Remembering every detail of the day a year ago. All my memories of what we had said and done. It was horrible, reliving the nightmare of our lives. I hated it and just wanted the day to be over but I didn't want to go into the second year of living without her. It was too far from the last time I saw her.

I arranged to meet Abigail's friends at nine thirty pm on the promenade in Thurso. About forty of them arrived, her closest friends. I took a bag full of candles for all of us. We each lit one and put it on the ground in front of us. One of Abigail's friends played a song on their ipod, it was a tough one. The song was about how they never got to say goodbye, they're missing her and how she never got to twenty one. Some of them asked for it to stop while others liked it. I personally find it tough but it symbolises exactly how we all felt. So many of the words relate to Abigail and how we feel. One of her friends has put it on the internet accompanied by photos of Abigail and messages to her. It always makes me cry when I watch it.

It began to rain but we all still stood there in silence and waited for our candles to go out. That's when I noticed a difference in some of her friends. It was that moment when it hit so many of us. She's really gone. She's never coming back.

A few ran off, some cried, we hugged. This was tough for all of us. I invited them back to our house. I went after those that had left; they needed a cuddle, someone to hold onto, someone to talk to. I think they were worried about upsetting me by saying how they really felt. But I felt the same; I knew what they were going through. I understood their pain. It was Ok to scream and cry, to shout and be angry. They could do it all with me and eventually they did. For lots of us, that's the day our grieving really started.

'Grieving is a process we all have to go through'

Injustice of Life

I feel really guilty as I remember the thoughts and feelings I had towards elderly people, for what seems like quite a long time.

As I look back I can recall driving past the old people's home and wondering 'Why? Why are they all here? Why are they all still alive and my Abigail's gone?' I would think to myself 'You could take ten of them instead of my Abigail. They've all lived their life, they've had a good run at it, but my Abigail only got fifteen years. It's just not fair. Take them instead.'

I would walk past people in the street or see them in the supermarket, complaining about nothing. Whinging and moaning just for the sake of it. Walking around with faces like thunder, miserable. I would wonder to myself 'Why are you here? What are they here to learn or teach in this world?' I would look down on them in disgust thinking, 'Just get a life. Get on with it or die. Stop being so bloody horrible to everyone.'

I even looked at my own Nan who I love dearly and I'm sorry to say I wondered why she was still here. My Nan was eighty years old at the time and is still going strong today. She's had her life. When I told my Mum how I was feeling and that I couldn't get these awful thoughts out of my head, she told me that my Nan had said to her,

'Why don't they take me instead? I've had my life. Look at me I'm all old and wrinkly,' as my Nan pulled at her wrinkled skin on her arms. I hadn't realised she felt the same too.

I later learned that most elderly people ask the same question when they hear of a young person being taken from this world, and young doesn't mean a teenager, I understand it can be anyone at all younger than them, from the generation below them downward.

I have tarred all old people as horrible here and yet I know this is not the case. Some are wonderful, loving and funny. I love to hear their stories of life, so different to my own. What it was like growing up through the war time, the experience of being evacuated. Their lives in general are a story to be heard with lessons we can all learn. To be grateful for the things we have, that we all take for granted. Even the simple everyday things like a having a toilet in our own home, yet nowadays we have several!

Abigail was always laughing, smiling, a happy-go-lucky person. She would lift the spirits of those around her, making them laugh and smile too. But these miserable old buggers would get me down and drain my energy. Surely Abigail deserved to be here more than them. She is worth a thousand old people and more to me.

But who am I to make this judgment? Nobody. It's not up to me or anyone else to decide who gets the chance to live or die. We all have a life to lead and a life purpose to fulfill. We are here for our length of time. Maybe we decide just how long we will be here before we come into this life. Who really knows?

'Life for some is too long and for others too short,

it just doesn't seem fair'

Legal Proceedings

I felt let down by so many of the professional services that were available to us. It's amazing I'm still standing today with the added stress some of them gave us over the twenty months following Abigail's death, before finally coming to trial at the High Court in Inverness on 1st June 2009.

Scott pleaded "Not Guilty" to Death by Dangerous Driving but asked for the lesser plea of Careless Driving. I was outraged. I still don't understand why he wasn't advised to plead guilty to Death by Dangerous Driving. He knew he had killed my daughter. He could have received a much lesser sentence for pleading guilty and wouldn't have put us all through further living hell.

* * *

Ruth our liaison officer began to keep in contact with us less frequently. Inside I was a trembling wreck all the time but on the outside everyone seemed to think I was strong and would comment on how well I was coping. I wasn't. I just held it together in front of so many, so yes it would seem I was Ok when reality was I lived in a daze struggling with each and every day. It's understandable then that Ruth also thought I was alright and doing really well. She felt she wasn't needed. I would have liked to hear from her more often than I did. It was always nice just to hear her voice, to know that someone from the police was there for us, she was our link with the legal proceedings, of which we felt we had so little information. One evening months after the accident I called the police station for information that I felt we should have been told. I went mad; I threw the book at the Sergeant on duty. There seemed to be a catalogue of events where Paul and I felt the whole system failed us.

Within minutes he had called Ruth who then called me to apologise, she thought I was Ok and didn't need her. The Sergeant came to our home to listen to all the issues we had, he talked us through a lot of the processes again. There was so much information at the beginning, we couldn't possibly take it all in and needed some of it repeated to us. We really needed their support. We talked at length, he stayed for hours. I met with Ruth at the police station where she was based for tea, it was nice to catch up with her and we still keep in touch today.

* * *

I remember returning home after Christmas 2008, having run away and spent time in Austria, only to find a letter, telling us that Tyrone was not being prosecuted. Paul and I were extremely angry at Tyrone to the point where I wanted to get in my car find him and beat the living daylights out of him. But I was also angry at the fact we had been sent a letter dated Christmas Eve. Did they have no compassion? Had this decision been made that day? I doubt it.

Paul and I wandered the house fuming, unable to calm ourselves or each other. We got in our car and drove round to our friend's Gary and Janet before we did anything stupid. They took us in, listened to us blast all our anger and frustration out until we finally calmed down; no physical anger left, too exhausted. Looking back we put our friends through hell. It can't have been easy for anyone watching us, to see what really goes on behind closed doors.

The next day I arranged to meet with the person who sent us the letter. I was so irate at their timing. I calmly walked into the office with Paul. We sat and I asked my questions, getting angrier and angrier with each of their responses. They didn't seem to understand that they'd done anything wrong. I was fuming.

I asked if the decision not to prosecute Tyrone was actually made on Christmas Eve. I was so angry with him. I shouted and swore lots, all of which didn't help. But, I was of course so irate.

Christmas for us without Abigail was absolutely unbearable and I told them this.

I stood up and shouted 'All you did was paper shuffling on Christmas Eve and finished off outstanding work that should have been done weeks earlier.' I stormed out, slamming doors behind me, probably swearing and shouting during my exit.

I'm not proud of what or how I reacted that day, but I certainly don't regret it. I was pushed beyond any reasonable limits. A matter of weeks later I received a five page letter stating in a lot of fancy words that my behaviour was inappropriate!

The letter was sent by someone we had met the year before. They had forgot to pass on our telephone number to Victim Support back then, a vital mistake with horrendous consequences for us, all because of their "inappropriate action" and yet they had the audacity to send me this letter. Their actions led to Paul and I being told on our doorstep late in the evening of the first court hearing that Scott had made no plea or declaration. We were told that Victim Support would call us. We should have received that phone call hours earlier and had unnecessarily spent all day feeling sick waiting to hear from them.

The officer being young and probably inexperienced gave us the news in the street for all to hear, not that anyone was passing, but that's not the point. We had asked on at least three occasions for him to come in. We had waited all day for the phone call from Victim Support that of course never came because they weren't given our number.

These are all supposed to be highly educated professionals. Bitter? Yes, I still am!

* * *

They didn't have enough evidence to prosecute Tyrone. Without the evidence I understand he cannot be prosecuted. This doesn't make it easier though. In fact it infuriates me, makes my blood boil. He was a witness in court, something I found very difficult to handle. I wrote to the Scottish Lord Advocate to explain how I felt about this and to ask if they had enough evidence without Tyrone's statement so that they could relinquish him from being used as a witness in this case.

I received a lovely reply from her offices and am grateful for the tone of her letter, explaining the circumstances. I understand why he was a witness.

* * *

Ruth our police family liaison officer introduced us to someone from Victim Support, who on our first meeting seemed very professional and explained the process of the court proceedings to us. Having left us with so many leaflets, we felt we had the support we needed to deal with the court case.

Boy, how wrong we were. Little did we realise how much distress and anger this person would cause us over the coming year or so. Every week when the case was deferred we would receive a call from them to tell us what had happened. Usually just to say that the case had been deferred again along with the date of the next hearing. We were always waiting to hear Scott's plea but the case was always deferred.

Week after week, month after month. Initially Paul and I both took unpaid leave from work and Hannah would have the day off school for each of these hearings. We would go out for the day, just drive anywhere leaving Caithness behind us. We were unable to cope with being at home or anywhere for that matter. We just wanted to escape. We never knew what to do with ourselves, just wanting the day to be over. We didn't want to relive those first few days and weeks in our head over and over again.

Eventually I used to take the day off on my own and paint the living room. A different colour each time, didn't matter what colour, it could never stay the same because it had been painted on a court day. I didn't want it as a memory in my face every day but I needed something to do and painting seemed to relax me, it was something I enjoyed. My living room went from cream to orange then purple. Week in week out a different colour. When the case was finally over I decorated it properly.

Stress running through my body, completely drenched in physical agony, nothing could take my pain away. It is unbelievable to even imagine that when Scott finally made his plea it was "Not Guilty" and the person from Victim Support remarkably decided to withhold this information from me when they called. I found out two days later when at Maria's house I read about it in the local paper. Unbelievable. I instantly thought the paper must be wrong because of what we had been told. I called the fiscal's office, eventually I was put through to the Tain office. The lady on the phone asked if I was Scott's mother. How seriously unprofessional are these people? Do they ever listen? I had already explained who I was. I was fuming.

Scott's mother had unfortunately passed away a matter of months after Abigail. I felt for his family at the time and had lit a candle for her on the day of her funeral, but to me it was outrageous to ask if I was her now. I was shocked and disgusted at the way I was being treated, passed from pillar to post. More than two hours later I finally received a call to confirm that yes Scott had pleaded, "Not Guilty." I was devastated.

How could they have done this to us? It was bad enough hearing his plea but to be treated in such a manner by those who were supposed to be supporting us was just ludicrous, a shambles. Even after writing a letter of complaint, I received little support, in fact only excuses and to be told how wonderful the staff are at doing their job. Yeah right! Obviously I still disagree with their statement. I would call to complain but no-one available to speak to me, instead I was told to put it in writing. It took weeks, sometimes over a month for me to write a letter as I had to relive all my pain. It felt so cruel.

There seemed to be a catalogue of failures. In some ways I'm sure it would have been much easier to not have them around. Some don't seem to have a clue about what information is really important to those of us living with this. No-one seemed to understand the process from our side; the victim's family.

There was only one gentleman, David, who throughout the whole process I trusted to give me all the information and be honest with us. Unfortunately he works part-time on a job share. I have met so many lovely police officers and professional people within Victim Support and other professional organisations, who I'm sure would have done a much better job. We just seemed to meet a few over this difficult time that we felt didn't help us or give a damn.

For over a year Paul and I said we would not be attending the court hearing if it ever went to court. But two weeks before the hearing I realised that I needed to be there for Abigail. Everybody in the car and witnesses would be in that court room. The prosecution would be there for the Crown. But for Abigail? There was nobody there for her. I didn't want to go and hear the events leading up to the end of my daughter's life in front of anyone especially not there, but I had to go, I had to be there for her. I arranged to go to court the week before when I was in Inverness so that I knew the layout and what to expect. It was agonising, knowing what I would be hearing the following week.

Paul and I stayed with our friends Maggie and Iain who live near Inverness for the duration of the court hearing. They were a great support to us, listening to what we went through each and every day, putting up with all our tears and anger, feeling our emotions with us. It was nice to arrive at their home at the end of each day. Even though each day felt like a week, I was exhausted, tired, stressed and helpless. I would let off steam, tell them what had happened, let it all out.

Then I would go and get changed, put on my jeans, have a glass of wine, a good long cry and try to be myself again for the evening. Try to laugh and chat about everyday normal things but it wasn't easy. Then the news would come on and we would all sit and look at the screen, staring at Abigail's photo on the TV. Listening in silence, tears would run; the pain always in my heart. Sometimes it just didn't feel real, like this wasn't really happening to us. We would sit in silence for a while; none of us really knew what to say for the next few minutes or so.

Each day I received so many texts from friends thinking of us, some would send lovely heartfelt messages, others just a 'x' not knowing what to say, which actually said so much to me and they knew this.

Paul and I sat through the entire court case, from selecting the jury through to the verdict. I remember when we first arrived my chest felt tight, sitting there looking at Scott. This was the first time I had seen him, the person responsible for taking my daughter's life. My chest in pain, I struggled to breathe. My body weak, already shattered before we'd begun the journey. I carried a box of tissues with me at all times. I knew I would cry and of course the tears ran and ran. I sobbed, staring at the young man who had destroyed all our lives. For what? A foolish mistake. David from Victim Support came over to us; he quietly whispered to me, 'Would you like to leave?'

I replied, 'No... Thank you.'

Moments later he came over again asking, 'Would you like a glass of water?'

Again I replied, 'No, thank you. I've got some,' and pointed to my bottle on the floor. Several minutes later he brought me a carrier bag. I looked at him strangely wondering what this was for? He pointed to the small mountain of tissues growing beside me. I hadn't realised, so many tears and snivels and I'd only been sitting there a short while. It was the same each day: another box of tissues. Every day we heard more evidence, the events leading up to that horrible accident. We heard Abigail's friends talking about what happened in the witness stand; expert witnesses calculating speeds and distances through to watching animated evidence. The final moments of our daughter's life. I gasped for air. I was in so much pain, I couldn't help but cry. This was the end. The moment that destroyed us all. I was watching the moment my daughter took her last breath. The moment she died.

I didn't sit in court to persuade the jurors or to get the sympathy vote. I seriously don't think I needed to. The evidence was clear. I sat there for Abigail and nobody else. Being there for her kept me strong.

Having been on jury service myself, I didn't envy any of them, this was a difficult case. Not tax evasion or fraud, someone, my daughter had had her life taken from her. I think it was a tough and emotional case for everyone sitting there.

Everyday when the court adjourned for lunch, Paul and I would usually walk down the high street to get a sandwich, not that we felt like eating. Chocolate and biscuits usually sufficed. But we needed to get out of the building even if only for some fresh air. We needed to escape. On the second day when we returned to the court room after lunch, Scott was already waiting outside with his solicitor and others. The door was locked. We stood and waited with David from Victim Support while someone went to get the key. I stood in a daze staring at the back of Scott's head. He killed my daughter. 'He killed Abigail,' was all that kept running through my mind over and over again. My chest crushing, my breathing changing, my body shaking inside - all the signs of a panic attack beginning. I couldn't move. David gently held my arm and walked me round the corner until Scott was out of sight.

'Are you Ok?' he asked.

Tears in my eyes, 'I can't breathe,' I replied holding onto my chest, 'but I'll be alright. God that was tough.'

'Tomorrow I'll check the door is open before you arrive,' he offered.

'No,' I said, 'I have to deal with this. It's better for me to keep seeing him here with all of you around me. I need to be able to cope if I bump into him in the supermarket or in the street. It will get easier. I have to face this.'

His face was surprised, 'You're brave.'

I'm surprised and pleased to say that the media were very good to us; they didn't approach us directly, not even when they filmed us leaving court. Instead, the press asked Victim Support if we would give an interview. 'No,' was my response. I felt this wasn't news, it was our life and how on earth would I answer any of their questions? I was an emotional wreck. But when I thought about it, I realised that although they were being nice to us outside the court, they may not be quite so nice when sat outside our home. I didn't want Hannah to return home from school to news reporters, journalists or camera crew sitting there. I was told by Victim Support that if we gave a statement it was likely they would leave us alone. So, I agreed to give a statement when the case was over but no interview.

Next thing to worry about: what on earth would I say? As if I didn't have enough to think about. Wide awake, another sleepless night. Three o'clock the following morning I sat and wrote my statement. Lying awake I'd been thinking about how I would feel if Scott was found guilty or not guilty and feeling all the emotions that came with both verdicts. I knew I wasn't going to be jumping for joy with a guilty verdict, nothing changes for us, our life is still the same. Abigail's not coming home. I knew that I couldn't write a statement straight after the verdict. I needed to be ready beforehand.

On the Friday morning, the last day of that awful week, it was suspected that the jury might come to a decision that day. Paul and I went into the local supermarket to buy a bottle of whisky and some flowers for the Victim Support staff who had all been so lovely to us that week. It may be their job to support us but it can't be easy to witness what we went through each day in private behind closed doors. When I arrived at the counter the lady looked up at me, smiled and asked, 'Are you going to a wedding?' I looked smart and wore a pink flower everyday to court for Abigail.

I smiled and replied, 'That would be a lovely thing to be doing today.' As we left I squeezed Paul's hand and said 'If only she knew. She may see us on the news tonight when I give my statement and kick herself. But she won't know just how much what she said means to me.' I'm pleased she thought I looked like I was going to a wedding. She made me feel good for just a few minutes. She made my day.

The verdict came in later that morning. Scott was found guilty by majority of "Death by Dangerous Driving."

We returned to our room within the court. I had to get ready to give my statement to the press. I read it aloud again, trying to prepare myself, trying to hold it all together. I looked in the mirror, thought I looked Ok. The best I could. Paul and I walked onto the steps outside the High Court. Cameras are not allowed inside the building so here we stood. My hands trembling, barely able to hold the piece of paper with my writing on. 'Breathe Nicola breathe' is what I kept telling myself. Nicola McAlly the reporter from STV News approached and asked if I was ready. She told me to take my time. The sound man stood by my side, camera not in my face thank goodness. The freelance reporter stood to the other side a few steps down with his Dictaphone. I read my statement:

"Scott's actions took Abigail's life away from her, and took Abigail from all of us. She will never get to fulfil her dreams and ambitions, she had so many.

We knew from the beginning of these court proceedings that no matter what the result, our daughter Abigail is never coming home and as for how we feel, there are no words to describe the immense pain in our hearts. We miss Abigail so much every single day and we will for the rest of our lives."

When I saw the news that night and my photo in the papers the next day I couldn't believe how terrible I looked. The sheer agony leading up to and living through the case had taken its toll on me. I was a mess, weeks without sleep, a continuous flow of tears, the stress of it all. I was a state, puffy eyed and exhausted. But at least now the case was finally over.

I had previously written a letter asking for it to be passed onto the judge after the court hearing. I wanted it to be read to Scott at his sentencing. I had asked for Scott to be given a shorter prison sentence if found guilty as I did and still believe that a long prison sentence was not the answer to all of this.

I understand that in the eyes of the law Scott needed to be punished and to deter others from making the same mistake. But I feared that if Scott spent too long in prison it was more likely that he would come out a different person and possibly into a life of crime. I didn't want that for him. I also believed that our community needed to see him released sooner as I hoped Scott would personally feel that he had not paid a high enough price and that the community would feel this too.

Punishing himself would be far harder than anyone else's. I also asked for Scott to give up something very precious to him, not a life like Abigail's but something symbolic and important to him, maybe a football. To never kick a football for the rest of his life in memory of Abigail would have meant the world to me. I asked that Scott be banned from driving for a very long time. I knew that they would not ban for life but I strongly believed he shouldn't drive again. Maybe he will decide this for himself. I don't want him to suffer the same as we have. The most important thing I asked for, was for lessons to be learnt. I hope that one day Scott will volunteer to go to Thurso and Wick High Schools for one day a year, to stand in front of the school and say, 'I fucked up and this is what I did.' If it makes one young person realise what they are actually doing when they learn to drive, it's worth it, even to the point where I would stand by Scott's side. If together we could make a difference, for others to learn by these mistakes, it might just save someone's life. I know that this in itself will be very difficult, maybe even impossible, but for me it's a more worthwhile punishment than any prison sentence.

We didn't attend the sentencing in court in Edinburgh. We didn't need to. Whatever he got wouldn't bring Abigail back. Nothing would make me feel better. There is no justice for her life. I later learnt from Victim Support that my letter wasn't read in court. This is apparently not something they do. I wish they'd told me earlier. There was no animosity in my letter, no hate. Scott is suffering too, I knew that.

On the day of Scott's sentencing we drove to Essex to go to my dad's surprise sixtieth birthday party the following day. We pulled over when we got the call to inform us of the outcome. Scott was sentenced to two and a half years in prison and a seven year driving ban, the most anyone has heard of. We sat in silence for a while before continuing our journey. I didn't sleep much that night, my thoughts with Scott. His first night in prison.

I was told he was taken to an adult prison for the first night and would be transferred to a young offenders prison the following morning. I felt so sad for him. What must he be going through? How scary it must have been. This wasn't the life his parents wanted for him, it was horrible. I know people probably expected me to be pleased, that he got what he deserved. But I wasn't.

I wanted it all to just go away and life to go back to the way it used to be; Abigail here and Scott living his life, free. But that's not to be. Scott had lost his mum and I felt for him and his family. It was a horrible day, trying to be happy and getting ready for my dad's party but all I could think of was Scott. Where was he? Hoping he was Ok, that it wasn't as bad as I imagined.

Don't get me wrong, Scott needed to go to prison for what he'd done. Others need to learn from his mistakes, and the legal system needs to show that people can't make these mistakes and get away with it. But it doesn't stop me feeling for him at times too.

Of Scott's two and a half year prison sentence he was released after just nine months and was then on Tag for a further six months. To begin with I found nine months to be difficult and very hard to handle. A whole year out of his life would have been more acceptable. To miss birthdays, Christmas, family occasions, but this was not to be.

However the timing of his release and Tag just seemed appropriate. Scott was released from prison a matter of days before his twenty first birthday just days before Abigail's eighteenth. He couldn't go out and celebrate as he was on Tag which means he had to be home from early evening until morning.

I'd organised a road safety campaign with the Chief Inspector of Police and the John O'Groat Journal. The local shops had decorated their windows pink. Scott returned home to memories of Abigail everywhere. I hadn't planned it this way and it couldn't have been easy for him. Scott's Tag was finally removed a matter of days before the anniversary of Abigail's passing in October. Sometimes I feel that things do happen for a reason and this is one of those moments.

'There is no justice for Life'

Stress and Shock

Stress and shock can lead you to do the strangest things, so out of character. Snapping at strangers for no apparent reason. Walking along the street and suddenly bursting into tears; telling complete strangers your life story and feeling like you have known them forever.

There are also physical symptoms to shock. My body would physically ache from head to toe, complete agony. I'd feel so heavy I wouldn't be able to stand, my legs like a solid oak tree trunk rooted deep beneath the earth, not moving an inch. My arms so heavy, as though my hands were hanging to the ground. As though they were the weight of huge great boulders that my body couldn't possibly carry. My head would feel like it was being crushed, enormous amounts of pressure squashing my brain so hard. My stomach empty, nauseous, dizzy, like the world was spinning around me so fast, my body throbbing all over. I would be howling inside while the outside looked vacant as if it didn't even exist. My life felt like it was over, what was the point of going on? I couldn't move, numb is an understatement. I felt dead, gone. My heart still beating and my lungs still breathing, living in hell, not being allowed to leave this world.

I would search inside myself, wondering why?
Why did this happen to us?
What did I do wrong?
Why Abigail?
Why my baby?

What did she do? And so on and so on......

Nothing is the answer. Nothing that could possibly deserve this. It's true what they say, like the song goes, only the good die young. You never hear of someone horrible that passes away, you only hear of the good ones; the ones that stand out, those that are always so happy and bubbly, always smiling, those that truly touched people's lives. This makes me proud; my daughter was one of these wonderful people, so maybe this is my answer. She went because she is and was so wonderful, that she was needed in another place where she can help others. She has completed what she needed to do here on earth and it was time for her to move on, to progress to better things.

When someone close to you leaves, you endlessly search for answers. Answers we don't have, none of us do. Some turn to religion, to faith, while others hit the downward spiral of deep depression and lose their soul forever. I feel like I've done it all. Been there and am now entitled to wear the t-shirt as they say! It doesn't mean I have any answers, I just know what comforts me. Where I have found answers that I can accept, understand and most of all live with. It has been a difficult journey of soul searching; immense pain that my words don't really describe that well. I can give you a picture but unless you've lived this, you really have no idea what it feels like; 'completely flattened' would be one pale attempt at description. You can multiply what you think this must feel like by a million and you don't even touch the surface.

It's about coming to terms with waking up in the morning, getting out of bed and putting one foot in front of the other. Knowing that yes, today I have to live again, I have to continue breathing, for what reason I don't know. I have come to understand that it is either live or die and it will be a very slow and painful death. One I know that Abigail wouldn't want me to have, but at the same time, I know I have to do this first and foremost, for myself. So I get up. I walk the path in a forward direction. I am going to live, to complete my life purpose, whatever that maybe. I hope that when I die, people will remember me for who I am and not that lady whose daughter was killed in a car accident. This isn't something you can come to terms with overnight and if anyone had told me this I would have probably screamed that I wanted to die. This has been a natural progression for myself, for my soul searching, looking for answers.

'Life is like a Butterfly,

so spread your wings and fly'

Insurance

We were told that we could make a claim to Scott's car insurance company for what had happened to Abigail, but initially we weren't interested. It wasn't until I was asked why I have car insurance and when going through my explanation I realised that yes we probably should make a claim. There is no sum of money that can ever compensate for the loss of a loved one, everyone is priceless.

I would rather be over a million pounds in debt for the rest of my life, living in a grubby horrible squat with cockroaches and have my daughter here with me. Of course we all would. I would happily put myself through hell for her to come home again. But I am living in what feels like hell sometimes because I am left here without her.

I made the call to our home insurance company, I had taken out legal cover with our buildings and contents insurance. They dealt with everything from there; they allocated a solicitor to us from Edinburgh. I explained to him on several occasions that really I have no interest in the money. I am claiming because that is one of the reasons why we have to have car insurance by law. When it came to figures our solicitor knew not to even bother telling me. There was no amount of money that would ever be enough for my daughter, no compensation.

It took me quite a while to come to grips with this, how would I handle whatever the figure was? It wouldn't be enough for Abigail and one day a cheque would come through the door but I had already been through so much pain and anger that I wasn't sure I could cope with this either.

After the court case and Scott was found guilty the ball started rolling with the insurance company and our solicitor was very good. I had asked not to be kept informed of the details of the claim. What difference did it make? None. I felt haggling over what we could and couldn't claim for was of no interest to me. At the end of the day the solicitor and insurance company would agree a figure and I didn't need or want to be involved. It would only upset me and make me angry. I didn't see it as money, it certainly wasn't something any of us could get excited about, there was no 'Yippee lets book a holiday,' it was to us just another formality. We were legally entitled to make a claim and so we did.

When the cheque did arrive, I sat and cried, all the emotions, the raw pain brought to the forefront once again. The pain never goes away but some days are better than others.

Our next dilemma, what on earth do we do with it? We didn't feel like it was ours. We hadn't earnt it. Abigail paid the highest price, her life. Here we were sat with a cheque. We saw it as Abigail's money. Then we asked ourselves what would Abigail have spent it on; probably blown it all enjoying herself; make up, clothes etc. One thing is for sure it would have been nice things and she would have had fun.

Paul and I decided we would give ourselves a small amount each to spend on anything we liked. I spent mine on a trip to Orkney, to buy a lovely necklace made with mother of pearl which has two doves in flight and I love it. Hannah chose a laptop and Paul got a tattoo, something he has always wanted and Abigail had suggested as a father's day present once. Each special in its own way to us and which make us smile, just like Abigail.

We moved to Cyprus and blew the rest trying to having fun!

'One day we will be together again,

but not today'

Moving On

When people say the term "Move on" to me, it stirs up so many emotions and feelings. My stomach ties in knots, twisted inside, angry even. Why would I want to "Move on?"

When you have an argument with someone, you want to forget about it and move on. Leaving behind all the stuff you rowed about and the emotions that came with it. So why on earth would I want to "Move on" from the tremendous pain I feel for the loss of my daughter? I don't want to forget about her, leave behind the enormous chapter in my life that she filled. Nor do I even want to leave behind my emotions, they show just how much I love her, care for her and miss her. So no I don't want to move on.

But, I do want to get up and live my life. To be happy, laugh and smile; of course I do. But move on, never. I'm not sitting around feeling sorry for myself or looking for the sympathy vote. The most horrendous thing that could happen to any parent or family has happened to mine, but I don't need or want people to feel sorry for me or us. I don't want people to look at us and think what an awful life we have been handed. In fact the opposite, so many wonderful things have happened in my life and Abigail was a huge part of that, along with her sister, my younger daughter Hannah.

So, moving to Cyprus, everyone thought and so many said 'How wonderful it is that you can move on and start a new life.'

'Oh bollocks,' is what I thought and in fact often said. Moving abroad or anywhere to be honest is not "Moving on" or starting a "New Life." We have just dealt with the pain and emotions attached to the house and area we lived in and decided it was time for change. The stuff going on in my head and heart hasn't suddenly disappeared or been washed away with a house move. Living in the sunshine, doesn't take any of that away. The pain will remain with me for the rest of my life and that's exactly where it should be. This is my life.

It took me a very long time to deal with the attachment to my home in Caithness. This was our last family home, where the four of us had lived together. It was our dream home that we had all longed for and worked hard to achieve. Yet having only lived there for a week before Abigail's tragic accident it still felt like our family home. I didn't know how to leave it. I searched locally and on the internet, viewing properties online that I could call home, none were suitable, none were our house.

Until one day, while shopping in Inverness we decided to go and view some new houses that were being built. The first real viewings as I hadn't wanted to waste anyone's time.

'Wow,' is all I can say. The house we saw was stunning, it was perfect, tears welled up in my eyes. This house was beautiful, the perfect family home. Abigail would have loved it. Paul saw me and was concerned, he knew we couldn't afford this house.

I think it took a while for Paul to realise that although this house had the wow factor, a real dream home in an ideal world, the reality of my emotions towards it had shown me the most important factor of all, I could move. I could leave our current family home and live somewhere else. We just had to find the right property and area. The search was on.

I searched online all over the UK, different places that we had liked on our travels, but nothing felt right. Paul and I had often talked about moving abroad when the girls had grown up and left home. Why not now we wondered? We both thought probably Spain or Portugal but hadn't seriously ever looked. Then on several occasions Cyprus was suggested to me, in fact one medium had told me, 'Don't worry when you move to Cyprus, Abigail will still be with you.'

I remember laughing and saying 'Cyprus.... I've no intention of living there.'

'Oh well maybe you will go on holiday there,' she replied.

I thought to myself, that's not likely either, Cyprus is for old people! Apologies to all those that live there because I now know that isn't true.

So having been told on at least three occasions that I will be living in Cyprus I decided to look it up on the internet and see what Cyprus had to offer and then cross it off the list so that I could get on with my serious search. The photos looked lovely. The kind of pictures in my head of where I would like to live and reading on, it seemed to tick all the boxes for what we wanted. I called out to Paul and Hannah from our garden room where I had been searching online, 'What's on your list of must haves?' They rattled off a few before I told them to come and have a look at what I had found. The more I researched Cyprus the more it seemed to create boxes and tick them too. I asked Paul,

'So, where did you think we would move to if we were to go abroad?'

'Spain or Portugal,' was his reply.

'That's what I thought too,' I said.

So I set about searching these as well. Within a matter of minutes we could tell that neither of these were what we were looking for. I love the Spanish language and found it relatively easy to understand when I had worked in Barcelona and Madrid so I just assumed that we would settle there. But no, not to be. We decided that if we still felt the same about moving to Cyprus in a few months time we would book a fortnight's holiday to go and see for ourselves.

Sure enough two months later we decided it was time for a change and booked two weeks in February, the cold and rainy season in Cyprus. I didn't want us to go and see it when it was lovely, in dreamy mode, we needed reality. We boarded the plane in Glasgow, one of the worst winters Scotland had seen for a while. Thick snow on the ground and freezing temperatures.

We got off the plane the other end of our journey late in the evening. My god it was cold. Not snowing fair enough, but cold and windy. I remember thinking as I walked down the steps off the plane, 'I'm not living here.'

Having already searched the local school options for Hannah online the only contender was the International School of Paphos. As Hannah was thirteen at the time we felt it would be too much of a struggle for her to go to a Cypriot school, not knowing the language and coming up to her teenage years where she would need to study for exams. We felt it best for her to go to an English speaking school that studied IGCSE's. We also didn't know how long we would stay. There was the possibility this could be an enormous mistake and we'd need to turn round and go home. We needed to know that her education wouldn't be affected too much.

I had pre-arranged for Hannah to sit entrance exams two days after our arrival, what an awful Mum! Three hours we left her there sitting Maths and English papers while Paul and I drove around the local area within commuting distance. But nowhere felt like home, it didn't feel right at all. I wasn't happy and we were not going to be living here. When we returned to pick Hannah up we toured the school. It's completely different to schools in the UK. The majority of classrooms seemed to lead to the outside, great in the summer. But a bit chilly it seemed in the winter months, wrapped up in my coat and scarf. All seemed very professional and a very good school. But, when we left the three of us discussed the school and the area and none of us felt this was right for us. So, we decided it was time to have a holiday instead and forget the whole idea of moving abroad.

It is amazing the people you meet in life and the directions they may send you in without them even realising. While now in holiday mode, window shopping in the local complex to our hotel I spotted a handbag with a picture on the front taken from a photograph. It was a personalised gift shop that made gifts from photos, either your own or they could take pictures of you. I really wanted one of the handbags and I had the perfect photo of Hannah to go on the bag.

We returned to the shop about five times, they were in the process of moving so were often shut while organising the relocation. The owner's daughter Millie was very polite and helpful and I later found out desperate to help as she kept calling her Mum to get back to the shop to make the bag for me.

Eventually I met Mo and Nick the owners. What a lovely family they are - very friendly and helpful. I never thought for one second that they would become our best friends in Cyprus and now they have moved back to the UK we still keep in touch, friends for life. In fact Hannah and Millie are off to the theatre in London next week as I write this. Anyway while in the shop sorting out my handbag Mo and I were discussing living in Cyprus. I explained that we had been looking for a school and home etc. Then Mo mentioned St. Georges Educational Institute at the Sea Caves near Coral Bay. She gave me their business card and told us how much Millie loved the school.

The next morning I called the school and spoke to one of the Directors and asked if we could make an appointment to meet them and see the school. There are no entrance exams here; your child is expected to attend the school for a three day trial. What a brilliant idea, an assessment on both sides. Hannah could get to see if she liked the school and the children too. We arranged for Hannah to start the following day. Initially it was suggested that Hannah attended when we moved to Cyprus. I explained that we may not move if we don't like the school.

I knew instantly that I liked it as I walked up the driveway. It felt right immediately. I just had to wait and see what Paul and Hannah thought.

At the end of day one, Hannah left the school very quiet, I had to ask a thousand and one questions to find out what she did and how she felt. Paul and I had spent the day driving around the area and working out budgets for the cost of living in Cyprus.

Day two was completely different. Paul and I went to view properties in the local area and found a house that we loved and could afford to rent. It seemed perfect and minutes away from the school. Hannah came out of school a different person, full of smiles and excitement, she jumped in the car and said, 'I love it, can we move here? I really want to go to this school.' Paul and I couldn't believe it. In one day we had found a home and school. Everything seemed to be in place and felt right for all of us.

Still not really wanting to jump in feet first though we went away and discussed all our options, thoughts and feelings towards the whole move. Should we stay or should we go? We really didn't know. Back in our hotel room I tore three small pieces of paper and wrote four choices on them all: Thurso, UK, Cyprus or 'keep looking'. I gave each of us a piece of paper and a pen for us to tick our choices. This way none of us were trying to please each other by just agreeing with one another. This way we could say how we really felt. It turned out Hannah and I had both ticked Thurso and Cyprus. I had had enough of searching, for me this was it Cyprus or just stay put. Paul had ticked Cyprus and keep looking, as unbelievable as this may sound that was it decision made, Cyprus got three ticks and so the move was on.

We went back to the school and made the necessary arrangements for our return and went to sign the contracts for the house. It unfortunately fell through the day before we travelled home to Scotland. But hey we managed to find somewhere else the same day. This was obviously meant to be, the easiest move I have ever made and I have lived in over twenty homes. We rented our house in Caithness to a lovely family. We sold our furniture and belongings, gave stuff away, stored items that we didn't want to get rid of in my mum and Weyland's loft. We packed up the essentials we felt we couldn't live without; all thirteen boxes including the barbeque and shipped them out.

We changed our mind about the date to move several times and eventually I said I couldn't leave before Abigail's eighteenth birthday, I just couldn't go. I had began to make arrangements for her birthday and I wanted to see them through.

On the night of Abigail's eighteenth birthday we went to the Comm, the Commercial Pub in town to say goodbye to all our friends before we left for Cyprus the next day. I couldn't call it a party because it was Abigail's birthday. To me it was just a drink down the pub with our close friends. I was amazed with myself that there hadn't been anywhere near as many tears as I had expected. Today I felt Ok. I had worked hard to organise the day and the move; I was ready to go.

With an enormous hangover the next morning we were delayed leaving. My head pounding, it just wanted to stay on the pillow. I eventually surfaced sometime in the afternoon and was disappointed with myself, as I had been so determined not to get that drunk as I didn't want a hangover. I had felt fine the night before. I could recall the whole wonderful evening. I later found out Scott the owner had been serving me doubles all night, cheers Scotty!!

We planned to stay with friends and family before we flew to Cyprus so that we could say goodbye. Our flight from Inverness to Luton had been cancelled in the morning due to the ash cloud from the volcano in Iceland. The airport had no idea when flights would resume, they told us it could be a few days. We had to get to Luton to collect our hire car and get our flight to Cyprus two days later so I phoned round all the car hire companies who didn't have a single car available. Eventually one gentleman joked and said, 'But I do have a van.'

Laughing I asked, 'Does it have three seats?'

'Yes.'

'We'll take it, when can we come and get it?' I asked.

Within the hour we were at last on the road, nothing was going to stop us. Even the little hiccups seemed to go smoothly and stress free, the move to Cyprus felt like it was meant to be and we were on our way.

'You get out of life what you put into it,

not what you take from it'

Abigail's 18th Birthday

Abigail had been talking about what she would like to do to celebrate her eighteenth birthday ever since she was thirteen. She said it gave her five years to plan and save up for it. Originally the plan was to go to New York, not just for three nights but a whole week she said. There is just too much to see and do. She had planned shopping for most of the time. She also loved the theatre; we would often go when we lived in Essex. "We Will Rock You" in London was our family favourite. Abigail was a member of the Queens Theatre Drama group when we lived in Essex. She loved dancing and acting and it was wonderful to see her confidence come on in leaps and bounds.

Now Abigail wasn't here and I didn't know what to do for her special birthday. She had wanted to do so many things and now she couldn't do any of them. I couldn't plan and work with her to make her day so amazing. We had already been talking about it for two years and here I was lost with nothing to plan and organise for her with three years ahead of me to face. Not knowing how I was going to deal with it.

I still needed to do something though, just like she was planning. Friends of ours suggested we went to New York as she had originally planned and enjoy it in her memory. But, I knew I couldn't do that. It would be too painful without her. To live her dream wasn't right, she should be living it, not me. Maybe I will go one day but not the year of her eighteenth.

A few months after her passing I decided to ask Thurso in Bloom if they would use pink flowers in their displays as a tribute to Abigail in 2010 for her eighteenth.

They are a local charity who brighten up the town with floral displays of hanging baskets and window boxes throughout the summer. I also wanted it to be in memory of all those who had lost their life in a road accident. To my surprise they agreed and in 2010 the streets were filled. They used lots of beautiful pink fuchsias; Abigail's favourite. She used to call them ballerinas like her Grandad Bob. I can remember Abigail explaining to me in great detail how plants reproduced while we were in a garden centre near Aldburgh where she chose a fuchsia for our garden - a funny memory which I wish I had paid more attention to at the time.

Lots of Abigail's friends organised a sponsored walk to raise funds for Thurso in Bloom. They all wore pink and looked amazing. Hannah took part and they walked the streets of Thurso. Originally they had wanted to walk from Thurso to Castletown. It's a dangerous road at the best of times and for me it felt like reliving Abigail's last journey. I was paranoid that something might happen to one of them so I persuaded them to change their plans and to walk around Thurso instead, going to places where Abigail used to meet and hang out with them. Many happy memories for all of them. Paul and I wanted to show our support and went to meet them all at the start with sweets for everyone. We met them all again at the end of their walk on Thurso beach.

My friend Lindsay who was also our County Commissioner for Girl Guiding organised a coffee morning with baking and book stalls to raise money for Thurso in Bloom and for "Thurso in Pink" for Abigail. Many of our friends helped and supported us. Jane from "The Flower Shop" in Thurso donated a beautiful modern pink floral arrangement as a raffle prize. I used to attend Jane's flower arranging classes. I always went on what I call the naughty table as I think I only copied her arrangement once. Her arrangements were always lovely but I always did my own interpretation, modern and a bit wild and wacky! She knew the kind of style I liked. It was so lovely, I wanted to win it myself! All the money raised went towards the additional costs for purchasing so many fuchsias for the town.

Leading up to Abigail's birthday, plans naturally began to grow and grow. Not only was Thurso going to have a beautiful floral display but I had also began to ask the local shop owners if they would have their window display's pink in her memory. Nearly every shop took part and the street looked amazing. Some had filled their windows with butterflies, others flowers and some with road safety advice. I remember one of the butcher shops telling me they would love to take part but didn't know what they could do; their window was filled with pink balloons. It was incredible to see on the day, the support we received was fantastic, "Thurso in Pink" for Abigail. She would have absolutely loved it. I made a photo thank you card for all the shops with a picture of Abigail and posted it through each of their doors in the morning before they opened. I wasn't sure if I could cope on this difficult day to actually walk the street and see their displays when they were open. The street would have been busy and filled with people, I would have felt everyone would be watching me.

I also organised a road safety campaign with the Chief Inspector of Police. The John O'Groat Journal agreed to print it on Abigail's birthday and surrounded the article in a pink border. Part of my statement to them said that I needed to ensure the importance of safe driving free from drugs and alcohol so that safe driving is a pleasure. But, also young drivers need to understand that once behind the wheel of a car their vehicle can become a powerful weapon of destruction if not driven correctly or safely.

The John O'Groat Journal included photographs of us as a family along with my thank you card that I had given to all those that supported us. The article was brilliant, a huge full page spread.

Thurso High School allowed the pupils to wear pink to school that day. Hannah told me that everywhere you looked someone was wearing pink. Wick hanging baskets, a community programme who organise floral displays for the town of Wick offered to have a pink floral display too. They created an area especially for local residents to go to where they could sit quietly and reflect.

The whole community of Caithness pulled together and it was a huge success. I had managed to organise something for her birthday that I would never have dreamt of doing if she were still here. "Thurso in Pink." It was perfect and I am honoured to have received the support that I did. Abigail touched so many and I think everyone wanted to be involved.

'We can still celebrate, even if only in memory'

Message to Scott

Before leaving Caithness to move to Cyprus I set up an account on a social networking site so that I could keep in touch with friends and family while living over there. I wish I had done it earlier while living in Scotland miles away from our friends and family in Essex. It's surprising how many friends you find you have!

Many of Abigail's friends sent friend requests to me, which I of course accepted. The website displays your mutual friends and on occasions I would notice that some of her friends were also friends with Scott. This used to break my heart; I couldn't understand how they could be his friend after what he had done. I found it so hard to deal with that in the end I felt it was best to remove them from my friends list. I sent each of them a private message to explain that I found it difficult. I still wanted to keep in touch with them and said that we could privately message each other. I liked to hear what they were up to, even though sometimes it was difficult.

From then on every time I received a friend request from one of Abigail's friends, I used to search for Scott and Tyrone to see if they were either of their friends first and if they were I would send a message explaining that I couldn't accept their request at that time. But in doing this I would of course see what Scott and Tyrone were up to; I didn't want to know. I didn't want to see that they were happily getting on with their lives like nothing had happened.

When it came nearer to Abigail's anniversary in 2010 I noticed that Scott had put a message on his wall looking forward to going for a drink the following Friday which was to celebrate his Tag being removed. This was the weekend before the anniversary of the accident. I felt sick to the pit of my stomach, angry and hurt that he was about to celebrate at a time when I was so distraught all over again. I was reliving and remembering all the pain inside and the loss of my daughter whom I so longed to come home. She should be out enjoying herself.

I read his message over and over again, day after day, the anger inside me growing with rage.

I wrote Scott a message on 22 September 2010 at 10:28pm:
'A day to celebrate your tag being taking off? You seem to have forgotten why you are wearing it. Did Abigail mean nothing to you? Only five days after your celebration is the 3rd anniversary of the day you took Abigail's life from her and destroyed all of ours. Something I certainly don't think is worth celebrating. Instead you should make others aware of the dangers of young foolishness. You could instead go to Thurso and Wick High Schools and explain what you did and try to save someone from making the same stupid and costly mistakes that you have, not drink the night away forgetting why.'

I didn't read through it again before I sent it, I was so angry. I clicked send. After I pressed the button I remember thinking 'Oh no. What have I done? How do I cope with a reply? What if he doesn't care and sends me a horrible message? What if he ignores me?' I logged off and wandered around the house, aimlessly worrying.

I was scared to log back on later that night in case there was a message. How could I read it? But how could I not? The list went on, but I needn't have worried. The following morning I logged in and saw he had replied to me twenty one minutes after I sent my message. I felt my heart stop, I froze. I plucked up the courage to click to open it. The tears ran, my heart sank and went out to Scott, he was sorry. The words he wrote to me were what I needed to hear.

Scott's reply 10.49pm:
'I'm so sorry for what I have done to you and your family, words can't describe how sorry I am and how bad I feel. It's on my mind everyday and I wish it was me that night instead. I never meant it to come across like I'm delighted. I haven't forgotten why I'm wearing it, and of course Abigail meant something to me. I know exactly when her anniversary is. I never meant for any of this to happen. All I was wanting to do was go and have a few drinks with my mates that's all.

Well I have been telling all my younger mates that have just passed their tests about it and for them not to do what I've gone and done. I just want to say again how sorry I am and I never meant anything bad about what I have put on the website.'

I didn't reply, there was nothing I could or wanted to say. I sat and cried for days, I had heard the word sorry direct from Scott, it actually meant the world to me.

'It helps to hear remorse'

Spiritual Awareness

Ok, so here goes. Time for the weird stuff! I've purposely put all this together in one chapter rather than thread it throughout my book; I wanted you to see that I am, to a certain degree a normal human being like everyone else. I live in this world alongside and with you all. I'm a parent who is grieving and always will be.

I have no specific religious connections or beliefs. I am open-minded and wonder if maybe we all believe in the same thing but just have different names for things. This is of course my own opinion and I wouldn't want to offend anyone.

I have a gift as do we all. When I was growing up I wasn't sure if it was a gift or a curse, scared most of the time by the feelings I would have. Things I could see and hear and those that I couldn't see but could sense. People weren't so open minded back then as they are nowadays and I had no one to talk to who could give me guidance or advice. My family all thought I was talking rubbish and just trying to scare them, so most of the time I lived in silence without any understanding. I wish I knew then what I know now.

I talked openly with my children when the subject arose about some of the things that happened to me. "Pretend friends" aren't always "pretend," but trying my best not to scare them, I wanted them to know that it was Ok, so that if they too felt or saw things, firstly that they wouldn't be scared and secondly they could at least talk to me without feeling that they would be ridiculed.

Abigail had a very special gift. When she was just two years old she spoke to my friend who had passed away, chatting to him in the corner of the room. I kept calling her and asked who she was speaking to.

'Rod,' she eventually replied. She was so engrossed in conversation, she placed her hands on her hips and said, 'You know, Roddy.'

She described him to me. This gave me great comfort; it was his way of letting me know he was alright. Roddy had been in a car accident when he was seven years old. I understand he was sitting on his Grandad's lap in the back seat. The accident had crushed him and he was left paralysed from the waist down. I had known Roddy since his late teens and so never knew him when he could walk.

I recalled a conversation I had had with him years earlier when he talked to me about being scared of dying. I remember telling him that I believed when he passed away he would return to when he was happiest. He told me this was when he could walk before the accident. Roddy was waiting for a kidney transplant when he passed away at the age of I think twenty four.

I asked Abigail if he was sitting or standing. 'Standing up,' she said.

'How big is he?' I asked. She held her hand just a few centimetres above her head. I was grateful for Abigail's gift as she could pass his message onto me. He was Ok. He had gone back to when he was younger and could walk again. I felt so pleased for him. Abigail could never remember the moment when we talked about it years later but she always found it exciting.

* * *

I remember one evening when we were living in Thurso, Abigail was about thirteen when she came home from a night out with her friends.

'Mum, you'll never guess what happened tonight,' she said excitedly as she rushed in the house.

I replied, 'No Abigail, what?' feeling her excitement, but imagining she was going to tell me about a boy she'd met.

She sat at the kitchen table and told me she had seen a ghost in the garages just round the corner from our house on her way home.

Amazed, I said, 'Really, what was it like!' Abigail went on to describe an old lady and I asked,

'What did you do?'

'Went back through to see if I could see her again,' she replied, 'but I didn't,' she said disappointedly.

I couldn't believe this. I was so surprised and told Abigail that I wouldn't have been able to go back, I would have been too scared. She just laughed and thought it was great. I was so pleased that she could come home and talk so freely to me without being worried what I would think.

So, the day after Abigail's passing when I felt her come home and cry out to me through thought, 'Mum, Mum, Mum I thought I was asleep, Mum I thought I was asleep,' I understood. I cried, it was upsetting, so emotional, but it also comforted me. Abigail could come home, to me her Mum. I couldn't hear her voice aloud, it's like hearing thoughts that aren't my own, I could hear the tone of her own voice in my head. I know it sounds bizarre but that's what happened. I have often heard from people who have crossed over in the same way.

I was worried though, thinking she might be all alone. Abigail didn't know anyone on the other side; no one had passed away in her life time that she really knew.

I know that many people are sceptical about spirits, ghosts etc, because it seems so scary. It's the unknown after all and very difficult to prove. I would describe these phenomena as energy. Imagine you are sitting in a room alone and someone was standing behind you, you didn't hear them enter but you knew they were there. You could sense them and if you know the person you would probably be able to say who it was too. What you can feel is their energy. When I feel Abigail I am sensing her energy and because she's my daughter of course I know who she is, so I know its Abigail.

If you rub your hands together to create friction and slowly move your hands backwards and forwards as if clapping very slowly but without touching you can feel the energy created from the friction. You can move your hands around and play with the energy, it's a wonderful feeling. If you can accept this and then open your mind to the possibility of similar things happening on a much larger, wider scale then maybe you can understand and accept that when we pass away, it's our bodies, our shell that dies. But our spirit, the energy within us lives on. I think it's something either we get and accept or we don't. I'm not trying to convince anyone, we all have our own beliefs and opinions.

So in the following days and weeks after Abigail's passing many things were happening to me, I thought I could feel Abigail, but I was also sceptical. What if I was going mad? My forehead would itch and sometimes I'd feel a burning sensation. I would get tingles up and down my legs. Every night when I went to bed it would feel as though my pyjama trouser would be moving like it was being shaken. I kept asking Paul if he could feel this, but no, he couldn't. I started to see people's faces whenever I closed my eyes; I felt so many spirits were trying to connect with me, one after the other and very, very quickly. I was scared. I didn't know what was happening to me. Was it Abigail? Had I opened a huge door and let so many other spirits in? And then was I blocking them because they were scaring me which meant I might be blocking Abigail too. I felt she needed me but I needed her too. I didn't know what to think or feel. I am a grieving Mum and didn't want to latch on to these phenomena without really knowing if it was my daughter. But if Abigail needed me, I needed to be there for her.

I remember going to Cawdor Castle with Paul and Hannah for the day near Inverness in Scotland. It's a beautiful castle and has a wonderful feeling inside. When I came to the yellow living room I stood for quite some time just looking at the room. It felt so homely and welcoming as if someone had just got up and left. I read the information board and kept being drawn to look at one of the portraits on the wall. I smiled to myself as I could sense the lady's presence. I felt her wrap herself around me to comfort me. She knew I was grieving and just wanted me to know that Abigail was alright, that she was with me. It's difficult to describe how I get these feelings but I have learnt to just follow my intuition and go with what I feel, it's like I just know. I smiled to myself and felt comforted. Paul looked over at me and I told him what had happened, what I'd felt. He's never shocked when I tell him stories like this anymore. He's never ridiculed me; he just accepted and knew that I found peace from it. I stayed in the room for quite some time; I didn't want to leave.

I would often feel Abigail around me and sometimes even kiss me on my cheek; it felt just like a little tickle. I would sense that she had gone to be with her friends who were still alive. I knew who she was with. It was like she wanted me to know where she was, like she would when she was here. There were two friends in particular I could sense her go to the most and one day I asked each of them if they ever felt Abigail was with them. I wasn't surprised when they answered yes. I wasn't quite sure how to ask to begin with and decided to just come out and ask them.

It was lovely to hear their stories of what they were feeling. One told me she always dreamt about a robin and its voice was Abigail's. I was overwhelmed and delighted. I told her the story of my great grandad whom I was very close to and how ever since he passed away whenever I see a robin in my garden I think of him. It's funny how I would always see a robin the day I moved into a new house, no matter what time of year it was. In our last house in Scotland we had two robins. We always thought of these as my great grandad and Abigail together showing us that they were Ok.

I feel that Abigail's passing has made my openness to spirituality leapfrog into worlds beyond reality; I enjoy it and welcome it with open arms now.

* * *

Since moving to Cyprus I'm surprised at how many spiritual people I've met from all different walks of life with different experiences and beliefs. I was obviously meant to be here to grow from within. I've met people who work with angels, energy and various types of healing to name but a few. I'm enjoying observing and learning, broadening my understanding of the world beyond what we can touch, see and smell.

I have completed a "33 days to transform you life" course that I thought would help me deal with my pain and emotions related to Abigail. But actually I have cleared out so much mental and physical clutter from as far back as my childhood and events that have occurred throughout my life.

When I finished the course I went to sit in nature, to just be alone. I thought about everything I had completed over the last month, meditating and focusing on different stages.

I sat on the rocks near the shore by Coral Bay looking out towards the sea, taking in my surroundings and feeling at one with nature. Just observing. I noticed the sun beaming directly above me with a scattering of clouds either side, watching as their shapes changed I felt as though I was surrounded by angels. Suddenly one of the clouds was changing shape very quickly, I thought this looks like one of the Gods, but who is it? The name Zeus immediately came into my head; it was a very moving sensation. He stayed there for ages, not changing at all. I had this overpowering feeling that I didn't have the whole picture and needed to turn around. I rose to my feet and as I stood there I felt absolutely incredible. As I turned I was astonished to see the whole sky behind me dark, dense and black. Completely full of dark rumbling clouds, still and silent, not moving an inch and here I was standing in beautiful sunshine. My Storm literally behind me! I smiled, held out my arms and felt free.

The path has cleared ready for the next steps in my life. I will always be grieving, this I will do until the day I go home to Abigail. But it's now time to be me. I know I'm weird but my feet are firmly on the ground!

'I love my Spirituality, I love who I am'

Healing

The day Paul and I went to Inverness to identify Abigail I found a "Lighthouse Healing'' business card in my coat pocket, a natural clairvoyant and healer. My friend Debs had given it to me several weeks beforehand. I remember tearing it up and throwing it in the road telling Paul, 'I don't need that. That's the last thing I want right now.'

But after five or so weeks of so many strange and unusual things occurring, I needed to go and find out what was going on. Was I going mad? I just wanted to grieve for my daughter and not hang on to any of this. Especially if it was all just in my head. I needed to know that Abigail was at peace, that she was alright and that I wasn't going off my trolley. As any parent will know and understand, we all worry about our children. What are they up to? Who are they with? Are they Ok? Are they safe? And so on and so on. Well for me that still hasn't changed. She may not be with us in person, but I still worry and hope that she's alright.

I spoke to Paul about what was happening to me; he didn't feel any strange phenomena but accepted that I did. I think he was worried about me and didn't want me to see a clairvoyant, which is understandable. I explained what I was looking for. I didn't want to have a reading or hear from Abigail necessarily. I wanted to understand what I was experiencing and to know that what I was going through was normal. I wanted to be able to accept and learn how to deal with it, even if that meant it was all a load of rubbish and nothing was actually happening. But at least I would know. Paul has since said to me if I wasn't weird before he would have been more worried.

I told my friend Katrina about the strange things that had been happening; the feelings I was getting, the touches on my skin. I could hear Abigail speaking to me in thought. I needed help; I needed to know I wasn't going doolally. I wondered if the clairvoyant, Christine, in John O'Groats could help me. I couldn't believe it when Katrina told me she had an appointment with her later that week. Katrina offered to speak to her for me to see if what I was going through was normal.

After Katrina's reading; she had explained to Christine that her friend had lost a child and that I needed to understand what was going on around me. Christine felt Abigail and described her and how she passed, as well as describing me; a lady with short red spiky hair is not your average looking Mum! Everything she said was accurate and not all in the press. Christine asked if I would go and see her for a chat, she wanted to help me.

Still sceptical as to whether or not this person could help but also a believer I called and made an appointment. I went along worried and anxious, a bit apprehensive at not knowing what to expect. I sensed Abigail feeling excited, 'She's coming, she's coming.' I needn't have worried. Christine opened the front door and welcomed me into her home. She gave me a very warm hearted hug and I instantly felt at ease. A tall lady with beautiful long dark hair, a roundish face with a beaming smile, warmth in her eyes, kind and loving inside and out; not "Gypsy Rose Lee" like at all.

She is a wonderful lady who has become a very close family friend.

Abigail came through to Christine and told me what happened that night. There were no surprises for me when I sat in the court room twenty months later. I had already heard everything from Abigail. Still, it didn't make it any easier but also it didn't make it more difficult by not knowing.

When I left after our first meeting I was in so much physical pain. It ran through my whole body and became more intense down one side, across my back and my head hurt so much, I was in agony. It wasn't until I reached Dunnet just before I drove through Castletown on my way home that I realised I was feeling what Abigail's body had suffered. Her body's physical pain. When I arrived home I needed to lie down, unable to sit and eat my dinner, I was exhausted. Thankfully it wasn't long before the pain passed.

Christine sat and listened to me without forcing any of her beliefs on me. I can safely say hand on heart she has helped me more than anyone else. I really don't know where I would be today without her. I owe Christine my life.

My meetings were like counselling really. I didn't go to hear from Abigail, but it was nice when I did. I always said Abigail could come home to me; I would just need to learn how to hear her properly. I didn't want to know my future, I didn't really care back then about a future. Most of the time I just wanted to die, so that I could be with Abigail. I needed someone to talk to who understood and didn't judge me, Christine was that someone.

I would often see rainbow lights twinkling across the room, around Christine and on the photos of Abigail I'd given her. I would sometimes look over at Abigail's picture and know she was there. It brought warmth around my heart and would make me smile, wishing she was with me so that I could cuddle her once more.

After a few weeks Christine asked if I was ready for some healing. Wow, I suddenly felt peace. I would feel so relaxed and calm, it was lovely. I felt like I was in heaven.

I lay on the bed with a rose quartz in one hand, amethyst in the other and clear quartz placed at my feet. Christine would tell me to close my eyes, to take slow breaths in and out until I became relaxed. She would talk me through visualising a beautiful white healing light coming down from above and entering my body through the crown of my head. I could feel the healing sensation almost immediately and slowly it would travel through my whole body. I felt peace. Embraced and surrounded by the glorious white light. I could see a stunning vibrant rainbow in my mind's eye leaving the soles of my feet and arcing up to the crown of my head. I could feel it remove my grief, cleanse my pain and turn into a wonderful healing energy as it re-entered my body. The powerful energy travelled in an enormous circle as it passed through me. It was such a beautiful feeling.

Once in this state of mind Christine would begin to talk me through a relaxing visualisation. My favourite was when I found myself on a beach, feeling the cool refreshing air on my face, the sun high in the sky and the warmth on my skin. I always imagined I was on a beach in John O'Groats, although I had never actually been to the beach I could see. I would watch myself walk over to an enormous rock, the only one there, thousands of years old. I would climb onto it and sit looking out to the horizon feeling completely grounded and at one with the earth. I watched the waves as they slowly rolled in front of me, listening to the beautiful calming sound of the sea. Not a care in the world, just at peace with myself; feeling totally relaxed. My body calm and my mind clear. Everything from the physical pain to the mind chatter where my thoughts just never seemed to stop had been cleared from my body. Leaving me in a completely clear and natural state. It must be how we are when we are first born.

Christine would then begin to start the healing. I could feel her touch my head, make swirling motions on my forehead and move her hands over me. I would begin to see colours behind my eyelids, mostly purple and green, swirling like the northern lights. My mind would wander back to my visualisation and I would slowly drift off into another world.

On one occasion I can recall meeting my guardian angel and being offered advice. All of this helped me. I was able to find understanding and peace within. Christine would bring me back to reality by stroking my cheek. Slowly I would open my eyes, back in the room, feeling calm and relaxed, serene.

We continued these sessions over a long period of time and each time I could feel an improvement within me. The experience was incredible; I could actually see my grief melting away.

Through healing, Christine has shown me the way so many times, giving me guidance, lifting me when I felt so low and life unbearable. She has also encouraged me to move forward at times when I thought impossible and most of all she has given me understanding. I often felt excited from the moment I woke when I was going to see her and this in itself has helped. To feel excitement when your body is riddled with grief is something you think will never happen. But somehow it does and it's pure pleasure. The sensation of feeling free.

Peace is a difficult word to describe unless you have truly experienced it. Nothing around you really seems to matter. Sometimes in a daze but completely comfortable with who you are and where you are in life. You notice the smallest of things around you; a walking ant, birds singing in the trees, the movement of the clouds or the trees moving in the wind. You become the observer. It's all wonderful, calming and nothing else matters. It can seem like a strange but sensational feeling, especially when you experience it for the first time, it's like euphoria. I wish I could feel this all the time, and the amazing thing is that no drugs or alcohol are required to get you there!

I asked Paul to come and meet Christine so that he knew what I was doing and that I wasn't hanging on to anything. I could sense that he was worried about me. So he came just the once to meet Christine. Now he understands that this is what I needed to do and that I haven't latched onto anything. None of this has taken over my life to the point where I am obsessed. My feet are firmly on the ground and I think I'm pretty level-headed most of the time.

I remember the first time I took Hannah with me, Paul was working late and I didn't want to leave her at home alone. She really didn't want to go. I think she was expecting Christine to be a witch of some kind and found the idea quite scary. I tried to explain that Christine and her husband were both normal lovely people, just like all our friends. If she saw Christine in the supermarket she wouldn't stand out like a sore thumb as someone who can hear from people who have passed away. When we arrived Christine gave Hannah a cuddle and made her feel welcome. I sat with Hannah in Christine's living room for a while until she felt safe and comfortable. I could see she was still a little nervous but she said she was Ok. Hannah sat and read her magazines while I went into the healing room.

As we drove away I laughed with Hannah, 'Do you really think I would take you somewhere scary to meet a witch?'

Hannah replied 'No,' and laughed. Hannah came with me on a few occasions after that and really likes Christine and Dave. They are normal after all!

I moved onto development work with Christine, to work on my own spiritual awareness. Christine would ask me to close my eyes and would place an object in my hand. Not really taking any notice of what the item was, I used to have to feel it within me. Pick up the energy and see what information I could get from it. I felt useless at times but I really enjoyed the experience. I would often come back to the room, open my eyes and say to Christine that I wasn't any good as I didn't really get much to tell her. She would hold up her notebook and show me the reams of information she had written from what I'd said. All true and quite exciting but it's not something I practice every day.

I enjoy looking at crystals and love having them around me. I'm drawn to them in shops and love to hold them, feeling their energy. It always amazes me when I read the meaning of the crystals that I feel I need. They always refer to exactly what's going on inside me. I don't believe I need to study them; I just go with my intuition which gives me a much better guide to what I need. I read angel cards which help to keep me focused and sometimes give my friends angel readings which they seem to enjoy.

I wanted to continue with the healing I received from Christine when I arrived in Cyprus but I was unsure who I could turn to. Nothing seemed to feel right for me so I decided it was time for me to learn to do this for myself. I heard about Reiki, a natural form of healing using universal energy, and I was drawn to it.

I searched online and found many Reiki Masters who taught within Paphos where I lived but my intuition told me that none of these were right for me. I knew for some reason that I wanted one-to-one training; I wasn't keen on other beginners practising their healing on me. Their energy may not be in line with my own and as I often think I'm a mess it was better for them not to have me practice on them either. I continued my search and found Angela in Maroni near Limassol. I booked a pulse healing session with her so that we could meet. I arrived at Angela's home to a very warm welcome from her and her dog. Angela is from Austria originally, a slim lady, with very long brown hair and a beautiful smile. The healing was lovely and we connected straightaway. I knew instantly that I could begin my journey into Reiki healing.

I booked my level one training a couple of months later and have never looked back. I remember when I first arrived Angela asked me, 'So, why do you want to learn Reiki?'

My response was, 'I feel completely selfish; I'm not planning to heal the world although that would be nice but I want to learn to heal myself.'

Angela smiled, I think she was delighted. We opened the training manual and the first thing she told me was the purpose of Usui's method of natural healing. Through the use of my own hands I could find my spiritual path to heal myself. I was so excited.

And so the training began, I spent the whole day looking at my life. I hadn't realised I, like most of us, have had so many things to deal with in life. From my childhood, my parents and family as well as employers. I began to notice a trend in the things I have done and situations that I always seem to end up in. But by accepting this as part of my life and my role within this I began to let go. It was like watching my own life unfold and realising my part in the things that have happened and just accept them. I was shocked at how easy it was to discuss my entire life with Angela. It was a very exhausting and emotional day but I watched my life change in front of me. It wasn't a huge effort to accept simple changes in my life and to realise who I am.

I learnt that Reiki is a form of universal energy that is channelled through us to help heal on a physical, mental, emotional and spiritual level. Reiki is the link between our physical and spiritual being. The energy doesn't drain our personal energy; in fact in practice I have noticed that it boosts mine. I am a channel to receive and pass on by allowing the energy to flow through me. We are all born with this energy as it is the energy of life itself.

After that initial session Angela told me I had to heal myself for twenty one days before I could return to complete the final part of my training. It was wonderful; I used to practice every morning usually before I even got out of bed. I would set my alarm early to begin with as it could take over an hour but before long I was naturally waking and starting my healing. Even Hannah noticed the difference in me. She said that I was much calmer, more chilled out. My sleeping improved and I watched the depression and sadness lift. My life had begun again!

It wasn't long before I progressed to level two and completed my Reiki Masters and noticed huge changes within me. Nothing really in practical terms initially but my outlook on life and what I wanted to do with it, where I wanted to go and the things I wanted to change.

I use Reiki in my life most days now, in one form or another. My attitude has changed and I am more accepting of what goes on around me. Through Reiki I have found that sometimes on sleepless nights when I'm feeling stressed I can lie in bed place my hands on my shoulders and by working with the universal energy I can easily fall into a deep sleep. When I wake I find my hands are still where I left them. It's a remarkable experience, a gift I treasure and am happy to share.

'Live everyday with joy and happiness in your heart'

Health and Fitness

Gaining nearly two stone over two years, feeling like a big fat blob I decided it was time to kick the weight off. I used to binge on chocolate, not just two or three packets of sweets but a coffee table full. One after the other I would eat them like they were going out of fashion. I didn't notice the taste or even enjoy them; they didn't make me feel good or full. I just ate and ate and ate. I would crave Chinese sweet and sour chicken balls with egg fried rice late at night. I would think nothing of jumping in my car at nearly midnight to go and get some. The weight just piled on.

A few months after the court case my life seemed to settle and I decided enough was enough. I hated myself, feeling fat and unattractive. I had put on so much weight, sometimes feeling low I would eat rubbish all night long. I went from one extreme to the other, all or nothing. In the first few months after Abigail's passing I lost weight and then it just piled on. Some days I didn't care and others I would hate myself but felt like I couldn't do anything about it.

I had just been food shopping and spent a small fortune when I finally made the decision it was time to do something about it and chose to start the LighterLife Light programme.

I called Ann from LighterLife and arranged to meet her the following day. Paul and I decided to do this together; he had gained a few pounds as well. We left Ann with a carrier bag each, full of a variety of uninviting packets of food. And so we started the LighterLife Light programme. We aimed to lose two stone each. It was quite easy actually, I didn't have to think about what to eat except for our evening meal. The tricky part was how to make a meal without carbohydrates, no rice, potatoes or pasta which seemed to make up every meal we ate. But it wasn't long before we made our food seem more interesting by adding different herbs and spices. The packet food wasn't too bad after all; I liked the cranberry cereal bars and milkshakes. Paul lost over eight pounds in his first week while I lost four and felt delighted. We were on the right path. Exercise wasn't allowed because we were on such a low calorie diet. Four and a half months later Paul and I had both shed two and a half stone each. I have never looked back. I feel great having gone from a size sixteen to now a size twelve and am still there nearly three years later.

I started to feel good, proud of myself and glad to be me. While on LighterLife I began to research moving to Cyprus, so the extra encouragement for me was that I would love to be able to wear a bikini and sure enough I do and feel great. Now years on from finishing my diet I eat normally and yes I eat chocolate, crisps etc, in reasonable moderation though. But now I also have the added enthusiasm of working out. I enjoy going to the gym and love yoga. So now I keep fit, eat what I enjoy and am alive, I'm back. Grieving, me, but yes I'm back.

In fact I think I have become a yoga junkie, I just can't get enough of it. I joined the Spa Tonic Gym in Coral Bay a month after moving to Cyprus. They have a huge variety of classes of which I probably attended more than half of them to begin with often spending more than three hours a day there while Hannah was at school and even returning in the afternoon after picking her up to go to Tai Chi. I felt great, alive and alert.

Mark, a personal trainer, has helped me to deal with some of my anger. I booked a one to one boxing session with him when I was feeling really angry with Scott and was finding it difficult to control. I explained to Mark that I wanted to beat the crap out of someone and felt that a lesson in a safe environment was a better idea. I thought he could definitely take my weakling punches. Mark's about six foot three and solid muscle. To be honest I thought I would probably throw one punch and end up on the floor in tears! I didn't. The session was great and when I feel anger building up inside me I book another session. Mark always makes me laugh too. I'm never angry by the time I finish. I'm too exhausted actually as it's a really good work out as well.

I have to say my two favourite classes though have to be Aqua aerobics and yoga. Aqua aerobics without a doubt is because Sue the instructor just has me in stitches from beginning to end. I'm sure my face gets a better workout than the rest of my body just from laughing so much and Sue has been a great support too. There aren't many instructors who would swim across the pool just to hold me when I'm sobbing in the corner trying my best to carry on working out while hearing the Christmas songs in the background. They brought back memories of all the things I would do with my girls. I was missing Abigail terribly and I couldn't hold back the tears. I was pain stricken living without her at one of the most difficult times of year when everyone else is happy and celebrating. The rest of the class were great too. I could see they were concerned but they didn't make a fuss of me, they knew I wouldn't want this; they left me to it and carried on while Sue just held me tight. Afterwards she apologised for playing songs that made me cry. I told her that if she had asked me beforehand I would have said that I would be Ok. But obviously I wasn't so even I don't know what's going to trigger me.

I absolutely love yoga. Heaven knows why when I look back to my very first class when Debbie at one point had us hanging upside down for what seemed like at least half an hour. I felt like a bat with my feet on the floor, stretching my legs slightly wider than hip distance apart, arms folded hanging under my head. God the pain running up my legs all the way to my bum. Then Debbie would say turn your toes out, then your heels, god the stretches went on like this till my feet were getting closer to either end of the mat, well not quite! Eventually we could bring our feet closer together and curl up to standing. Oh boy! Head rush, feeling dizzy and sick I wondered what the hell I was doing there. Was this really enjoyment? No just sheer pain. But I kept on going, returning twice a week for more of the same. The saying, "No pain, no gain" is so very true. I felt like I was being tortured at times. I was always pushing myself that little bit harder, I wanted to become fitter and more flexible. I have a back injury and often struggle with some of the exercises. I desperately wanted my back to get stronger so that I could flatten my tummy. I'm still working on it. Most women I meet would like a boob job, me a tummy tuck, I can live with no boobs but the big fat blob of a stomach still gets me down. It's well hidden under my clothes!

Twice this week I have been told 'You don't need to go to the gym you're so skinny,' Mmmm skinny, I don't think so.

My neighbour once said to me that I was a fitness freak. She quickly retracted as she meant to say fanatic, but then I haven't been fanatical about anything in my life. But I suppose I am now about my yoga practice. Vanessa another yoga instructor came to teach at the Spa Tonic, so now I attend three classes a week. Dave the owner, has often commented that I'm at the gym more than he is. It's probably true some days. Vanessa's yoga practice is completely different to Debbie's and I love them both in their own way. I have never been able to do a press-up in my life, but now I can. From having to do so many downward dogs, cobras and upward dogs my arms and my back have strengthened. I'm a lot more supple and can get into some really strange looking positions.

I remember while Vanessa was explaining how to get into a bird of paradise pose I started to follow her instructions. Before I knew it I was standing on one leg with my other leg tucked under my armpit, one arm wrapped around my leg and the other around my back with my hands clasped behind me. I could hear Vanessa tell me to ground my left leg to the floor, focus and stand up straight, I did it. Wow! Then I heard everyone clap, I looked round, dropped my leg and realised I was the only one in the class attempting the posture, we all laughed. I had to do the same again with the other leg now!

I find so many benefits to yoga, other than the strange positions I seem to end up in. I have learnt to really focus on my breath. By controlling this I can control most of my emotions and attitude to life. I can focus within myself and by starting my practice with just breathing it allows me to focus on the rest of my day.

I have on occasions found myself oblivious to where I am and my surroundings and have been sobbing in the darkness. Lying on my mat at the end of the class, lights either off or dimmed, my eyes closed. I'm in a completely relaxed state on the floor and here I find myself a mess. Uncontrollably crying and for no apparent reason; my grief releasing from my body. I felt great before I walked into the class and now all the emotions pouring out of me like water flowing from a jug. Vanessa explained to me that when we do hip opening postures it allows us to release our emotions. Well I have released a bucket load. Yoga has really helped me not only physically, now being able to do a press-up and my body more supple but also emotionally and spiritually. Most importantly is how I feel while at the class and for the rest of the day; my mind clear and at peace, connected with my spirituality, focused on my breathing. I feel energised and ready to face the world with a smile.

I am more connected with myself and have definitely become an addict. I would love now to progress my yoga practice and become a teacher myself. Bringing yoga fully into my everyday life and sharing it with others feels like heaven to me. I aspire to show others the benefits and to help them heal themselves. I maybe many years away from that but that's my focus. So watch out India, here I come for the next step on my spiritual path.

'Peace, love and harmony'

Emotional Mess

Some days are just horrendous and there is nothing you can do to change it. Take today for instance, November 2011. I woke up before six am and thought it was time to get back into writing this book. Unsure where to start, I started to read through from the beginning. Oh boy, I wish I hadn't. It wasn't long before I was sobbing; my eyes filled with tears. Finding it impossible to read anymore, I closed the laptop, leaving just my memories to contend with.

I decided I was going to get up and go to the gym and forget the bloody book. I only lasted about ten minutes on the treadmill. I lay on the mat and decided to do some sit-ups. I managed three or four, no enthusiasm or motivation in me. I just stayed there, flat on my back with tears in my eyes, unable to move. Not in the mood. I should just go home and have a soak in the bath is what I thought. Holding back the tears while driving, I walked in the door and broke down in a heap, bawling uncontrollably.

I slowly walked upstairs; my head hung low, feeling the heavy weight of climbing each step. I went into the bathroom and turned on the tap, poured the bubble bath and went into my bedroom to lie and wait. Time to chill out and relax, I thought. I turned on the laptop, my face solemn. With tears still in my eyes I began to read again. It's just one of those days, it's a bad one. The worst this year.

I crawled into the bath and melted under the hot water and foaming bubbles, but I could feel this wasn't going to work either. It didn't lift my spirits; I didn't feel all warm and comforted inside. The sobbing began and I just wanted to die. I wanted my life to be over. I wanted the pain to go away, it hurts so much. The emptiness inside, the pain in my heart. It's just too much to bear, my life felt like I was living in hell.

I pulled myself up and had a shower instead, hoping to wash away the heavy emotions of grief, let them all drain away. I collapsed and curled up in a heap in the bottom of the bath, I sobbed while the water poured over me. I screamed out, but nothing could help me. There was nobody there.

Feeling sick, I just wanted to throw up, but nothing. I longed for all this to go away. Four years on and I still have really awful days. I probably will forever.

In a state and not sure what to do with myself I sent my friend a text asking for help. I really needed a hug, someone to hold me tight, to help me let it all out. He replied, he would be with me in an hour. I could hardly wait. I pulled myself together, feeling light at the end of the tunnel. I could deal with the day, slowly.

I got dressed; too hot, too cold, jumper on, jumper off. I crawled into bed fully clothed and sat back at the laptop and decided to write this. The emotions of writing, it seems like hell sometimes.

A whole loo roll of tissue already used and its still only morning. But through experience I know that tomorrow will be a really good day and I will feel great having released all these emotions, letting it all out, I just need to get through it.

My friend didn't arrive. He text me two and a half hours later to say he had arrived at the gym and was sorry he was busy. He had a lot to do that day. I was devastated, I felt destroyed, he was the only person I had called for help. I lived just round the corner, less than a five minute drive. I didn't want to talk, there was nothing to say. I felt dreadful and just wanted a hug to help me release my pain, to sob in his arms. His actions pushed me just that bit further over the edge. Maybe he will never understand.

I thought I was meant to suffer alone. The day got worse as the hours went by. All I kept thinking was that I wanted to swim out to sea and never come back. I felt heartbroken.

Fortunately, I received a text from my friend Judy about midday to ask if I wanted to go out for lunch. Yes was my instant reply. She didn't know what I was going through that day but she gave me a focus, a purpose. I now had to sort myself out; I had to look presentable to go out. I changed my clothes, pulled myself together and put on my makeup. I had a lovely lunch and began to feel better being outside. When I returned home I walked through the front door and began to cry before I had even closed it behind me. The deep heart wrenching pain returned in a flash once I was alone.

At four in the afternoon the friend that I had text for help finally arrived to drop off the cat basket he had borrowed. He rang the door bell and walked away. I couldn't believe it. My heart sank again. I couldn't suffer anymore, I needed help. In desperation not to be alone I called my friend Clare. She came to get me without hesitation. In her car she held me in her arms while I cried my heart out. We sat there for about twenty minutes. I needed to release. Eventually I calmed and she took me to her home, the weight finally beginning to lift. She cooked me dinner and looked after me. Later that evening I received a text from my friend Heather asking if I was going to the quiz that night. We attended the quiz most Thursday nights. I called her and my friend Brenda and we decided to have a girlie night in together instead. I certainly wasn't in the mood for going to the quiz.

I was still feeling down in the dumps but surrounded by wonderful friends who rescued me. I will always be so grateful to them for dragging me out of today's black hole.

'You really know who your friends are in time of need,

remember, friendship is a two way thing'

Two Heads

I feel like I have two heads when trying to deal with my grief and the best way I think I can describe it funnily enough is to compare it with my hands.

When I bring both hands together, palms and fingers touching as if in prayer position my hands look as if they are one. This I think symbolises my everyday life. However when my hands are separated my left hand shows my spiritual side, where I feel I have understanding of where and why my daughter Abigail is where she is. I can accept that maybe she and I along with others agreed to this happening before we entered into this lifetime. Maybe so that we could learn the lessons we all needed to learn and for our souls to progress by living with these circumstances. I believe that Abigail is an older and wiser spirit than me and I am grateful that she chose me as her mum.

But when I look at my right hand I see the parent in me. The grieving, angry, sobbing, heartbroken Mum. I get angry with Abigail sometimes feeling really annoyed with her for getting in the car, for leaving me. So frustrated that she would do something so stupid and then I collapse, missing her. It's not her fault; I forgive her in an instant. I feel so much pain inside, unable to cope with day to day living at times. I long to be with my daughter, all I want is for this awful life of pain and misery to end. For the day I die to draw nearer.

As I cannot cope being only my right hand, one of two heads, I have to bring my hands together, in some form of harmony to enable me to get up and get on with each and every day. I lean more towards my spiritual side as this I feel I can cope with better; I can get up with ease and focus on my day, on my life.

I take each day as it comes, some are better than others, I try not to suppress my feelings but sometimes it's easier that way. To hide it all away. It's easy for others to think I am coping really well, when really all I'm doing is keeping my spiritual side stronger so that I can cope inside. The pain within won't disappear or dissolve, no one can make it all better. It's a case of knowing myself better than anyone else. I'm very self aware of who I am and how I cope and therefore know the answers that work best for me. Sounds easy I know, but I often make mistakes and come down with an enormously huge thud.

Take a step outside the box and look inwardly, what do you see? I see a sad and desperate person who wishes she had a magic wand or a time machine that could somehow make this all go away, to wake from this horrible nightmare and find it was all a dream. Yet I don't think that will happen. The reality is, I know it won't, but I am sure when the time comes for my life to end and I get to wherever it is that we go, I will say,

'Ah I get it now, send me back so I can get it right this time.'

'Being self aware

can help you find what you're looking for'

Abigail's idea of Heaven

Now I'm sure, only Abigail while studying standard grade RE would write how she really feels. I'm sure most of her class would have written something completely different when the task was set for them to write their idea of heaven the week before her passing. I love what Abigail wrote for it brings a smile to my heart every time I read it.

'Heaven is where clouds are made of every colour candy-floss, houses are made of marshmallows with chocolate button door bells and melted chocolate swimming pools and Jacuzzis.

There are lots of mini fluffy angels like wasps except they don't sting they kiss you.'

'Enjoy the magical moments of life,

for who knows what tomorrow might bring'

Memories

No matter how tough it may seem, sometimes memories are all that we have left after someone has left this world for the next. But often memories usually do one of two things. They either upset us because the painful memory of having to live without them cuts so deep or they make us smile till we laugh. These we treasure the most and welcome.

There is no way of knowing which way a memory will take us until we are in the moment. I often find other people's memories harder to deal with because for some of them I wasn't there; I missed the moment and can't share a happy memory of my own daughter.

But, I remember on Abigail's sixteenth birthday, the first one without her after the accident, Paul, Hannah and my mum and I arrived at the cemetery. We saw a group of her friends preparing their flowers for her grave. They saw us walk up and hurried themselves to leave. I wasn't sure if they were feeling like they shouldn't be there or just feeling awkward around us, but I encouraged them to stay. They had just as much right to be there as us. They were there to grieve for their friend, a person they were very close to and miss as much as we do.

We all stood there in silence for a moment then I asked them to share one of their happy memories of Abigail. It was nice to see some smile as they recalled their memory and retold their stories of the things Abigail used to get up to.

From messages she wrote on her friend's school books to her explanation of those big triangle things called pyramids!

Some of my favourite memories are of her smile, the dimple on her cheek and even the annoying ones where she would always have her thong on show where her hipster jeans were just that bit too low.

My favourite though is the way she would get over excited about the smallest of things, a bit like me to honest. And she is the only person I know who had favourite noises. Yes noises. Abigail's two most favourite were the sound of autumn leaves as they crumpled under her feet. She would walk along smiling and giggling to the sound and do it even more to hear them. The other was the sound of a cork being popped from a wine bottle when it's opened, not that I drink that much really! Abigail would put the cork back in just to hear it pop again. I smile whenever I hear these sounds as I think of Abigail.

I loved Abigail's skill to get her own way; she really knew how to play me. For instance I would come home from work to a beautiful sparkling home with that lovely fresh clean smell. Abigail knew I would be delighted and of course I would thank her. She would wait about half an hour until I had settled in at home and started dinner. She would come and sit in the kitchen to talk to me and tell me about her day all smiling and happy. Then she would talk about her plans for that evening with her friends. Explaining what they were all up to but of course she would have to be in earlier than everyone else. So, generally without her having to ask I would tell her she could stay out that little bit later. I was of course in a good mood. What a push over I was! But she knew how to play me, make me happy and she could have what she wanted within reason, but then she also knew not to push me too far because she wouldn't be allowed out at all. I always tried to be firm but fair.

I loved her smell. Her clothes in the cupboard even months later still smelt of Abigail. I miss her smell, she always smelt lovely. I would often go into her room and just hold her clothes to my face to feel as if she were in my arms. Cuddled to her smell. It was nice to think she was just at school or out with her friends and not really gone. I used to use her perfume sometimes just so her smell would linger around me all day. When Hannah and I had finished the bottle I bought another to replace it and kept it in Abigail's cupboard with the others.

I lost all my memories at the beginning and I needed to hear others to help trigger my own, it's nice to finally have my own back.

'Treasure special moments they become happy memories'

Relationships

In the early days I really didn't think Paul and I would make it through this together. It wasn't that I didn't love my husband; I just didn't want to be with anyone. All I wanted was to die. This wasn't fair on Paul or Hannah. I often thought about leaving, so that they could get on with their lives without me. I never once thought that if I left this would devastate them. I thought I was a nightmare to be around and they would be better off without me.

Paul and I grieve in different ways, we all do. Paul is quiet and keeps things to himself whereas I show my emotions. I scream and shout when I'm angry, I let it all out. I feel sorry for the person who is near me, which was usually Paul. I get in such a state, all worked up, unable to cope with the smallest of things and when I finish I collapse in a heap wishing I could control my feelings, wishing this would all just go away. Wishing I could be normal.

Before Abigail's passing Paul and I never really argued, not that I can remember. Maybe the odd row here and there over the years, but nothing major. In fact it was funny I remember our girls often coming into the kitchen while we were cooking dinner, they'd tell us to stop kissing and we would laugh. I used to ask them, 'Would you rather we argued all the time like some parents?'

'No,' they would giggle as they walked back out the door.

But after the first few months of shock and feeling stunned we began to argue, progressively getting worse. It was always over something really silly, just a misunderstanding that would blow completely out of proportion. This wasn't us and I hated it. Over time we came to realise this and talked about it, trying to work out triggers and what we could do to help each other. Neither of us wanted this. We loved each other and wanted our lives back the way they used to be. We knew this could never be but we needed to try our best.

Stress and grief takes its toll on your own physical and mental state. When everyone in the house is going through this, it's difficult to cope with anything. Our lives had been turned upside down. We wanted to be there for each other but needed to deal with our own emotions too.

Months and months had passed before Paul and I even thought about making love again. It was difficult. We would always stop in tears, unable to be happy, to feel pleasure. I would feel guilty, it wasn't right. We would lie in each other's arms crying, feeling each other's pain and sadness. It was a long time before we were really ready to fully enjoy again.

People say time is a great healer; bullshit. Time heals nothing at all. Hard work and determination to head in the right direction is what helps to heal, inner will power and the strength to carry on. I remember feeling like I was standing in a field in the open countryside, watching as the fast train whizzed past me. The train, my life. I would watch in a blur as it went past, unable to move, waiting to get back on. I felt that my train never slowed down enough. My life was over, stuck here in the field, alone.

But life goes on, whether we really want it to or not. Time doesn't stand still and wait for us; it passes us by without a care in the world. You can't turn it back and you can't move it forward, you can't see, touch or smell it, time just travels by.

Eventually having been through so much pain, letting everything out, trying to deal with and come to terms with the next steps in my life's journey, I wanted to get back on that train. But I needed it to slow down a little to fit my pace of life. I waited and eventually I was ready. Did time heal me, NO. I worked through the stuff in my head, slowly. I still am and always will be. We humans are like onions with plenty of layers. So thing's we think we have dealt with will I'm sure come back in another layer for us to deal with all over again. I don't think I will ever get on that fast train again, but that's alright, I'm happy where I am for now.

Since moving to Cyprus and with Paul working away for three weeks at a time then home for only a week I have had the space and time to deal with my emotions and grief on my own. I found things I really enjoy from meeting so many spiritual people here. I have learnt new skills such as reiki healing, yoga and encaustic art, all of which I love. Through doing all of this though I have had to look inwardly at myself, realising who I am and who I want to be.

The more I looked within me the more I realised I needed to make huge practical changes. I came to realise that Paul and I were now on separate paths, wanting different things from our lives. My spirituality is taking me on another journey in a different direction. Unfortunately I think this was the beginning of the end of my marriage. I could stay with Paul but I would feel like he is holding me back or I could go off like a rocket with him dragging behind. This wouldn't be fair for either of us and so it wasn't long after thinking it through and talking to Paul that I decided it was time for us to end. It was very difficult. I didn't want us to break up a few years down the line, to just go on living with each other knowing it wasn't right anymore. I didn't want us to end up hating each other because I wasn't living the life I wanted to. It seemed better to me to make the break now and continue to be good friends and wonderful parents together for Hannah.

Over the following weeks and months I felt confused as to whether or not I had made the right decision. I have lost the life Paul and I had planned together, a scary prospect feeling vulnerable and lost. Another form of grieving in its own way.

It wasn't my spirituality that caused this but the fact that I was able to look inwardly at myself and knew that I wanted to go off and do something different with my life. I'm not sure where I'm going now but I'm following my own path.

I don't for one minute regret our marriage. Paul and I have had a brilliant seventeen years together, many ups and downs and horrendous things to deal with. I continue to love Paul and always will. He has been my best friend for a long time, the one person who really knows me inside and out. We still get on really well; there is no animosity between us which is great for Hannah too. She says it's a bit awkward at times but that's it. I'm now finding the new me, an exciting and scary prospect, who knows what the future holds.

Hannah lives with me while Paul is working away and lives with her dad when he is home in Cyprus. Hannah seems to be coping extremely well with it all, she is very mature and accepting for her age. I on the other hand have been a quivering wreck completely unsure how to cope at times, realising I've made huge mistakes along the way and often feel like I'm the worst parent on earth by destroying Hannah's world even further.

I did meet someone else who turned my head and made it spin; it was like being in a whirlwind romance as the cliché says. Everything was wonderful to begin with, full of romance and excitement. But unfortunately within a couple of months I came to realise Steve is a drink driver and this in itself has been extremely difficult for me to cope with. I told him how I felt. But living in Cyprus I have noticed that an awful lot of people whether Cypriot or British tend to drink and drive and think it's Ok.

Slowly we destroyed our relationship. Looking back over the last several months it hasn't been an easy ride for either of us or our friends, who have been there to support us through the ups and downs.

I fell for Steve hook line and sinker. But at the time I was separating from my husband, trying to write my book, reliving my pain and still continuing to grieve. My life was in turmoil, yet here I was absolutely besotted and confused. Did I do the right thing? Sometimes I don't know, but life for Steve and I is no longer the same. Slowly we are bridging the gap that we created but at times we have struggled to even be friends.

Life is too short for all this stuff. I just want to be happy with some fun and excitement in my life again. Is that really too much to ask for?

'Life doesn't always run smoothly;

but try to enjoy it anyway'

Drink Driving

Scott hadn't had a drink when he picked Abigail and her friends up from Thurso, yet I have such difficulty with drink driving. I always have.

When I'm out at night or round at a friend's having a few drinks, people often ask me, 'Don't you drink?'

'Yes,' is my reply, 'but I'm driving.'

'Oh,' and then I get that look.

I'm happy to go out and drink water, lemonade or orange juice; I can still have fun without alcohol. I can drive home and am happy to drive my friends too. It's great to wake up without a sore head as well. It's nice to have a drink though. I really enjoy a glass of wine or two but Amaretto with lemonade is my favourite. It tastes like marzipan in a glass. But it's not essential for me to drink to have a good time.

People always assume it's because of what happened to Abigail that I have difficulty with drink and driving but it's not. It's because of what happened to her that I now struggle with it even more and find it very difficult to deal with. I know the pain and suffering any parent has to go through when this happens to their child or someone they love.

As people leave and get in their car, having had quite a few too many, either on their own, with friends or leave with their own children my body stiffens, I bite my tongue and say nothing, the pain and emotions rising up through me. I tense up and can feel angry towards them. They have no idea I feel this way. The thoughts, 'Please don't do this, just don't do it,' go through my mind, but I say nothing. It isn't my place to. Close friends and family know exactly how I feel because I tell them.

When I get home I feel sick to the pit of my stomach, worrying whether they got home safely, tears in my eyes reliving my own pain having to live without Abigail.

I don't sleep very well on those nights either. I wake up with horrendous nightmares recalling when the police officer knocked on my door and told me Abigail had died. Seeing the photo of Abigail's body in the car and then the worst, the vision of her body when I identified her, reliving the moment I stood there and had to say that this was my daughter.

This picture in my head won't leave me and I only relive it with drink driving. I wake up uncontrollably sobbing, unable to cope, unable to stop. Pain riddled throughout me. Remembering those most difficult first few weeks and reliving it all in my mind over and over again.

When someone drinks and drives within the legal limits I accept this. Whilst with Steve I even had a drink and drove home myself on occasions, I'm not proud of myself and look back with regret. I was influenced when I shouldn't have been, I should have been stronger.

I don't cope at all though with the actions of those that drink well above the legal limit and still think that it's alright to drive, convinced they are a safe driver. I'm sure they think they're invincible, but they're not, none of us are. People believe this will never happen to them. Please believe me, it does.

I wish that Abigail was the last person on earth to have lost her life in a road accident; that people would learn from what happened to her. Sadly she's not and I feel for all those families that are suffering too.

If only the memories in my head, the visions that I see could be erased. I just wish people would stop and realise the dangers they are putting themselves and others in.

Since moving to Cyprus I have struggled with this more than you could imagine, so many people here drink and drive. You won't believe how many people tell me they don't do it in the UK but they do it here. It's as if it's Ok. So the nightmares became more frequent. I have had to work hard to deal with this, trying to get it out of my head but I find it very difficult when I watch people leave the bar having had a few too many.

In trying to deal with all of this I have come to realise when my nightmares started, the visions I re-live after seeing people drink driving. It goes back to the day I heard Abigail's friend was caught drink driving at four am the morning after the hearing. I read about it in the local newspaper a few weeks later, it devastated me. It knocked me for six. The news of this at the time set me back months. It was like having to start my grieving process all over again, back to the day she died.

I bumped into the young lad months later in the local pub; I followed him to the smoking area and asked to talk to him. I was destroyed that he of all people hadn't learnt the lessons. Abigail thought the world of him and I know he did her too. He apologised to me and called himself some really horrible names. I know he regrets it and I believe him when he told me he would never do it again.

I know that he is struggling with what happened that night, we all are. But that's when my nightmares related to drink driving began. I can see that now.

'Living without someone you love

is the worst pain of all'

Christmas Celebrations

A matter of days before Christmas 2007 I feared the worst. How on earth are we going to deal with this? I didn't want to go to my Mum's for Christmas, the same as we had for many years while living in Caithness. But I didn't want to leave my Mum and Weyland on their own either.

I woke up early one morning just before the school Christmas holidays and sat with Hannah. I asked 'If you could go anywhere in the world for Christmas, where would you go?'

'I'd be with my cousin's Daniel and Oliver,' was her reply, 'but that can't happen.'

Hannah walked off into her room to get ready for school and I thought to myself why not? I phoned Paul at work and told him how I felt and what Hannah had said.

'Ok let's do it. I'll speak to my work,' he said.

I called my sister Vicky and explained that Hannah really wanted to be with Daniel and Oliver and asked if we could stay. Vicky's response was of course it wasn't a problem.

I went into Hannah's room and told her she could have her wish, we were going to stay with Vicky. She was surprised and delighted.

A few days later we made the very long journey, over six hundred miles, back to Essex, but feeling guilty that we had left my Mum and Weyland. They decided to open their Bed and Breakfast for Christmas. They didn't want to celebrate in the traditional way either.

There wasn't really enough room for us all at Vicky's so we stayed with my sister Lisa for the week instead. But on Christmas Eve we knew Hannah wanted to be with Daniel and Oliver. So Hannah went alone without us. We agreed with the children that they would wait for Paul and I to arrive the next morning before they opened their presents from Santa.

I lay in bed sobbing all night long with Paul. Not only our first Christmas without Abigail but also without Hannah under the same roof that night. It was tough. I don't think I slept at all. I wanted Hannah to be happy and have the nicest time she possibly could. For me, Christmas as we knew it was officially over. I haven't celebrated it the same since and probably never will.

We all went to Lisa and Casey's for Christmas dinner. That was extremely difficult too, everyone knew it was tough for us but it was also painful for them. Receiving gifts that they knew I had bought with Abigail earlier in the year. I was always organised early. Having us with them without her around had never happened before. Sitting at the dinner table, no seat for Abigail cut deep within me. I desperately wanted an empty seat there for her.

I was angry with Scott the driver, I wanted to send him a Christmas card telling him to make sure he had a chair at his table for Abigail. I wanted it to be in his face, there wasn't a place set in the world for her that Christmas and I couldn't bear it.

I received call after call on my mobile that afternoon from Abigail's friends. I was surprised they were thinking of me on Christmas day and phoning to see how I was. I sat at the top of the stairs in tears with Abigail's closest friend Sarah on the phone. She told me not to cry, that Abigail was still with me on Christmas day. It touched me so much that they were thinking of Abigail and thought of us too. I received lots of texts as well, friends telling me that they raised their glass to Abigail. People remembered her and knew it was a really difficult day for us. Our friends are so kind, they were there whenever we needed them.

* * *

Now our Christmases are different every year. From a skiing holiday in Soll, Austria to quad biking in the desert at Sharm el Sheikh. All fun, different, but most of all enjoyable. We've slowly learnt to take pleasure in Christmas again. We can't do our usual traditions on the day, or at least I can't. The only person I buy gifts for in December is Hannah. It's too horrible to walk around the shops with everyone in good spirit, excited about their celebrations when I can never celebrate the same again. Never able to buy Abigail a present yet seeing so many things she would have liked. Often stopping in a shop staring into space, thinking of Abigail. My eyes filled with tears, I would go home, forget the shopping and spend the rest of my day feeling miserable.

Hannah used to share Abigail's room with her on Christmas Eve so that they could open their Christmas stockings together in the morning. Just the two of them. I thought it was nice to have something special just for them. Plus it meant I didn't have to get up at some ridiculous hour in the morning. They used to come and wake Paul and I at about seven, showing us all their gifts. Silly things along with nice little presents like jewellery and perfume. We would then all go downstairs together to open the presents under the tree.

Hannah now sits on the sofa and opens her stocking with us. Things will never be the same again. None of our Christmases since have been easy, but we do celebrate. We try to enjoy ourselves; we just have to think out of the box a little and do it differently.

It becomes rather expensive trying to organise holidays at Christmas. This seems really unfair when all we are doing is running away from tradition. But in order to afford it we go without a summer holiday, go without luxuries and save during the year. I just have to get away from home. I can't bear the thought of waking up Christmas morning in my own home doing all the normal things, remembering the excitement on the girls' faces when they saw the huge pile of presents under the tree for them. Opening the gifts they thought they wouldn't get, seeing their pleasure. Hearing the girls laughing and enjoying their day so much. All of us smiling, happy, playing games, enjoying Christmas like any other family. But I can't do this anymore, I wake up and feel the sadness within me. The loneliness without her. The pain inside us all. Abigail should be there too. I knew one day they would grow up and do their own thing, but that will never happen now. Abigail was taken from us too early. We aren't spending Christmas without her through choice. We will never see Abigail again.

* * *

Austria was our first real run away Christmas in 2008. We booked a skiing holiday, something we had never done before. So, yes it was different, no memories here. I had fallen down the stairs and had a serious back injury which meant I was unable to ski. Great I didn't really fancy that part anyway. Lots of Gluhwien for me instead! It's like hot mulled wine but better.

So our first day, skiing lessons booked for Paul and Hannah. We collected their ski boots, skis and instructions and off we went. Paul's lessons were at the base of the mountain whereas Hannah's were half way up. I took Hannah up in the cable car, found where she was for the morning lesson and left her with the instructor.

Off I struggled in the snow finding it very difficult to walk with my back injury to the nearest bar for my Gluhwien. I walked into the restaurant and noticed an enclosed seating area at the end of the bar, a perfect place for me to sit alone without looking like a loner. I took off my coat and the many winter layers. I sat and ordered my drink. I heard James Blunt's 'You're Beautiful' start to play. Being emotional anyway at this time of year the tears were soon streaming down my face. I sent a text to my sisters and my friend Julie. I felt I was being punished for leaving home and then the next song on the radio was Robbie Williams, Angel. Both songs were played at Abigail's funeral. The poor lady behind the bar couldn't speak English. She saw that I was crying and brought over a huge pile of serviettes for me to wipe my tears. I was grateful; I sat there and let the tears flow. I heard those two songs over and over again that week. In the end they made me smile, Abigail must have been with us.

* * *

In the summer of 2009 I started planning where to go and what to do for Christmas,. Knowing that it had to be something different again, I searched online and spoke to friends about various ideas. The Creiff Hydro Hotel in Perth Scotland was suggested to us. I looked it up, read reviews on the tripadvisor website and thought it sounded a good idea. Paul and Hannah agreed.

Some of the reviews suggested that parts of the hotel were a little worn while others said how fantastic it was. I think they must have been in a slow process of upgrading all the rooms. I called them to find out how much it would be for the three of us. I explained the reviews on the internet and told the gentleman on the phone that I know he can't say any are horrible but could he please choose a really nice one for us. He laughed and talked about a few of the rooms, they all sounded lovely. I explained that at some point during Christmas day I might find it a bit difficult and would probably need to escape, I didn't want to ruin any other guests' day. After all they'd have paid a lot of money to enjoy their Christmas while we were running away. I ended up explaining about Abigail, not that I wanted to use this but felt it was easier to explain myself. He must have thought what a fussy lady!

He told me there was a new room that had just been refurbished and had become available for bookings; a two bedroom suite. It had two bathrooms, a small lounge area and at the end of the room a long tall window with a seating area looking out over the hills. It sounded perfect. The cost wasn't much more than a standard room. He said he would hold it for a few days for me so that I had time to speak to Paul and Hannah before booking. He was such a lovely man, who I never got to meet. Ten minutes later I called back and booked four nights.

It was the worst winter in Scotland for many years, so I was pleased we had booked our stay. Most people were unable to travel after Christmas due to the road conditions; it was a nightmare for them. But for us the scenery was beautiful, everywhere covered in thick fluffy snow. When we arrived we were assisted with our luggage. I told them our room number and his face beamed. I smiled and asked 'Is it nice?'

He grinned and said 'I'm sure you'll like it. Wait and see.'

We walked into the room. It was perfect, just what I needed. The gentleman looked at me and said 'It's nice isn't it?' I burst into tears. He must have thought stupid woman! We had the best room, every time room 333 was mentioned the staff would have this little glint in their eye and a cheeky grin. I later found out that there were three families already trying to book our room for the following Christmas.

We woke up on Christmas morning and sat at the end of our room looking out over the snowy hills while we opened our Christmas presents. No tree, just twinkly Christmas lights draped across Hannah's presents.

I pre-booked for us to go quad biking on Christmas morning, we rode along shallow icy rivers, it was brilliant. We all had a great time, lots of laughter. We went back to our room and watched a movie away from everyone else, munching jelly beans that had been left in our room for us. Christmas dinner was delicious, we had a great day. Of course we missed Abigail constantly, but we managed to get through it, which I don't think I could have done sitting at home.

We sat there on Boxing Day and I asked 'So, what shall we do next year then, snorkeling?' Paul and Hannah laughed.

* * *

Two months into the New Year of 2010 I started to think seriously about what to do for the next one. Somewhere warm would be nice, we had done the cold snow for two years. Sharm el Sheikh in Egypt it was. Maybe we would go snorkelling after all.

I used to find the 6th October; the date Abigail died impossible to read or write, I couldn't bear to look at it written down or hear it mentioned. The date would turn my stomach, make me feel sick to the pit of my stomach, just emptiness inside, my heart aching and wanting my world to end. This is why the date isn't written on Abigail's headstone. I couldn't cope with it, I hated it.

But now, it's a completely different story. Would you believe that this Christmas escape to Egypt finally enabled me to face this? The strangest things happen at odd times. Later in the year we decided to make the most of our Christmas holiday and go to Cairo and see the pyramids which has been a dream of mine since I was a child. Having heard many differing stories of Cairo I was unsure as to whether or not we as a family would all enjoy the city. I decided to book a really nice hotel so that if the worst came to the worst we could at least escape to luxury. I booked three nights at the Intercontinental and yes it was lovely.

When researching where we were staying and looking at different options for things to do I couldn't believe what I was reading. Near where we were staying was the 6th October bridge, then the 6th October town! My chest felt tight with anguish. At first I hated it and wished we were weren't going at all. I didn't think I would be able to cope with simply being there and thought it would bring on the most horrendous panic attacks.

For some reason though, the more I researched and read the date, the more I felt that I should go. I started to like it. The 6th October city was named after the 6th October war in 1973, which also happens to be the year I was born. A link between our lives: the beginning of mine and the end of Abigail's. It may seem farfetched to some but the date can now make me smile. It's part of Abigail and so it's part of me.

We arrived at Cairo airport, got a taxi after a fair amount of haggling and arguing. Would you believe about ten minutes later we were stuck in a traffic jam on the 6th October Bridge? Plenty of time for me to take photographs. It was very symbolic. If I hadn't discovered this earlier I'm not sure I would have been able to cope. But Abigail managed to be part of our holiday over the Christmas and New Year and I began to love the date as part of her life.

Paul and I separated in May 2011. This will probably be the toughest Christmas of all I thought. My first without either of my daughters and on my own. But I will deal with it. Paul's shifts meant that he was home for Christmas. Hannah is always with her dad when he's home. Paul's sister Carole, her husband Greg and their daughter Sophie were flying over to Cyprus to celebrate with them.

It would have been extremely unfair of me to expect Hannah to stay with me over the Christmas period and I knew she would have a great time with them all.

So, I flew back to London and stayed with my friends Mo and Nick and their families. They were so lovely and welcoming, allowing me to gatecrash their Christmas.

I was a mess, it was horrible and more than anything I was missing Hannah and Abigail. I was also missing Steve my boyfriend, who at the time had become an ex once again. We had been on and off so many times, but I missed him terribly and wanted to be with him on Christmas day. I had run away to escape, maybe I should have stayed in Cyprus after all. My emotions were all up in the air, unable to cope with anything.

Christmas morning I called Hannah, it was lovely to hear the excitement in her voice. She had a new phone and lots of other lovely gifts. Hannah and I had our Christmas day together two weeks earlier. We went on a helicopter flight over Paphos Harbour then out for a lovely meal just the two of us. It was a brilliant day out, but it still wasn't Christmas.

Then I called Steve, I was missing him and I felt so alone. We talked for a while wishing we were together, wishing we had worked things out. He sent me a text afterwards to say how lovely it was to hear my voice and then another text from him came through. It was a joke, I didn't realise this at first and then it dawned on me. I was distraught, devastated. He sent me a joke about drink driving. I know he meant well, it was supposed to be funny, but to me it wasn't. I cried uncontrollably, my day destroyed, I wanted my life to end. I couldn't cope and didn't want to live or feel like this anymore.

I didn't want to ruin my friend's Christmas day so I went for a walk. I wandered the streets in tears. My brother in law Barry had said to me the day before 'Nick why don't you go to church, some people get comfort from it?'

'Hmm, not for me,' I'd said to him.

But here I was Christmas morning wandering around on my own. I went to cross the road and as I looked down the street I saw a huge church. Barry's words rang through my head. I walked towards the church, up the stairs and before I knew it I was inside. Everyone was happy and singing, celebrating Christmas. I walked to the end of one of the pews, joined a lady and stood there crying. She put her arm around me.

I felt as though I was surrounded by angels, comforted inside. My pain began to lift. The service finished and I sat there not quite ready to leave. A lady came and joined me. She said to me,

'Sometimes we lose someone we love and we are missing them.' She paused. 'Sometimes we want to be with our loved ones and it's just not possible and sometimes we miss family, friends, husbands, boyfriends.'

I smiled at her and said, 'Try them all!' I missed everything and everyone at that moment. It felt like my life was over.

We sat and chatted for a while and she asked me if I would like to join the congregation for a glass of wine. I declined and sat there on my own for a while. She handed me a clean tissue and left.

Another lady came to join me. I cried; we talked through our lives. Before I knew it she was making me smile. I stayed so long we ended up sitting there in the pew with a glass of wine in our hands. The time passed really quickly, suddenly we realised everyone else had left. Boy did she help me that day. She walked with me back to Mo and Nick's house where I joined them all again and tried to continue with Christmas.

My mind would wander, my emotions a mess. He just couldn't understand how hurt I was. Christmas day is probably one of the toughest times of year for me, already emotional and extremely sensitive. I was struggling to hold it all together. Any other time of year I would have been annoyed, but that day it just destroyed me. I know looking back I blew it all out of proportion.

Nick's Christmas dinner was absolutely delicious; I have to say he makes the best gravy in the world. They have such a large family that the hustle and bustle of everyone enjoying themselves was a good distraction for me. More friends and family arrived, lots of singing and silly antics were on the cards for the rest of the evening. My thoughts would drift, still hurt and upset. I tried to hold it together but it was difficult, I was surrounded by so many people, yet I felt so alone.

I feel I ruined my friends' Christmas. They're kind enough to tell me that I didn't. But really and truthfully I shouldn't have gone and am sorry for spoiling their day.

Next Christmas who knows what I'll do? Las Vegas sounds like a plan to me!

'People say it gets easier,

but I'm not sure it ever will'

Hannah

Hannah is growing up fast; she was only ten when Abigail passed away. That seems such a long time ago now when I look at her maturing into a young lady like Abigail. Hannah is now fifteen, a scary thought remembering Abigail's last year at fifteen, but one I have to deal with. Sixteen is even scarier, a year older than Abigail. It's like the point of no return, Hannah will from then on always be older than her big sister. A thought that never occurs to you when you plan to have children, look to their futures and visualise them growing up together.

Hannah and Abigail like most siblings were always different from each other. Abigail was little miss chatterbox like me while Hannah was always the quiet one in comparison just like her dad. The house now seems so silent without Abigail.

I have no idea how Hannah really feels inside, fortunately I have both my sisters still with me. I have never lost a sibling. It must feel like losing the other half of you, but I can only assume. We often talk about Abigail, thinking about what she would be doing now, what she liked etc. But it's like Abigail can sometimes come alive for me when I see Hannah's natural reaction to some things or the faces she pulls, it's Abigail's mannerisms that come out. Of course Hannah isn't trying to be her sister, it's just natural and I love it. I will always smile and say to Hannah, 'That was just like Abigail,' and we share a laugh or smile together.

Hannah doesn't really show her emotions to me or her dad. She keeps them to herself. I have tried to get her to talk more about how she feels but I fear that she's afraid of upsetting me. We have talked about that too. I've explained that I'm always upset and that's Ok. My concern was always that she needed to release her feelings and talking is the easiest way to do this. Yes it brings up emotions, but that's good. It helps you to let go of some of the pain. I should know, I've done plenty of it!

Hannah is so considerate, a very mature young lady for her age. I can talk to her about how I feel. Not all of it, I don't want to hurt her either but some things I can say. She listens and always seems to answer with such maturity. I'm so proud of her.

It would have been so easy to either wrap Hannah up in cotton wool or the other extreme letting her go wild and live her life because for some of us it is far too short. But I believe we have done neither. Paul and I have always tried to maintain the "Normal" life we had before. Our same rules still apply. Sometimes I would make comparisons to Abigail and say to Hannah, 'No, I didn't let Abigail do that at your age,' and other times I've been a bit more lenient or harder, having learnt from my mistakes. They are both individuals too and can cope or react differently in different situations. So of course sometimes the rules are slightly different but not too drastic.

I have heard of some parents that throw money at their children, wanting to give them everything. They sometimes turn to drugs or crime, looking for and needing attention. While other children feel they are neglected. The parent is suffering so much that they have lost sight of the child or children they still have with them. I am conscious of this and feel I have always tried to keep Hannah's life as normal as possible. Yes at times I have been so distraught with grief that it's hard to maintain the normal family life while suffering.

When talking to people about Abigail it may seem that Hannah is left by the wayside but that's not my intention at all. When I finish I apologise to Hannah for this and she's always understanding and says it Ok, but it's too late I've done it. She knows how much I love her and that I miss Abigail too. She is very understanding.

We've talked about how I love both my children equally. It's not like when a second child is born your love splits in half so that the first now only gets a share of the love they used to have. You find you have the same amount and match it, always having equal amounts of love for them both. That doesn't change when one of them is gone either. I love both my children exactly the same amount: that will never change.

There isn't a training programme for parents, we learn by our mistakes and boy I have made some big ones along the way. I have regrets at the way I treated Abigail at times and do with Hannah too. But at the end of the day, it's a learning curve. I can apologise to Hannah when I make a mistake but I can't with Abigail. Some of them eat away at me but over time I have had to let go and just accept that if she was here I hope that she would understand and forgive me. Unfortunately that's the best I can do.

I know it will always be difficult living without Abigail for all of us. I am so glad that Hannah has such wonderful friends that she can turn to. None of this is easy for her either. I know that her friends from both Scotland and Cyprus have really been there for her at the most difficult of times. I've wished that she could talk to me, but I know that I've needed friends more than family too. They are often easier to talk to because they're not living with the pain as intensely and can often see things from an outsider's perspective, which always helps. Thank you to all of Hannah's friends who have been there for her. I will always be eternally grateful for the help and support they have given her.

'Sisters by Heart'

Writing

Writing this book was something I never planned to do. My friend and colleague Clare had suggested to me many times to keep a journal, to write down my thoughts and feelings. She thought it might help me to release the turbulent emotions I experienced every day. I didn't know if I was going to burst into tears or lash out at anytime but one thing was for sure, they came out. The pain, the tears and the anger. I showed it all. I didn't know how to keep it in. I would fly off the handle raging with emotion, the frustration inside me boiling over and then collapse in tears, crying uncontrollably, finally calming, everything released. Then I could continue with my day. Clare saw it all.

I was able to control myself with my clients. I was focused on them. But in between clients my thoughts returned to my life, my daughter. Often my clients knew Abigail and would talk about her. Clare and I tried to bring the conversation back to them often struggling as they needed to say how they felt. That was the trouble with living in such a small community; everyone knows everybody and all of their business too. My sister once told me it was like being with a celebrity, wherever I went people would come and speak to me or hug me. I couldn't go anywhere without being recognised. This in itself was comforting though, I wasn't alone. I had the support of a whole community who all listened when I needed them most.

Clare often suggested that I wrote a book about my feelings because I never hid them, I didn't pretend everything was Ok. I wasn't fine and would sometimes reply to people who asked, 'How are you?' 'Not good, it's a bad day,' or 'Fucking shit,' depending on how I felt or who the person was. The look on their face was a picture, but my attitude was if you don't want to know, don't ask. I couldn't say, 'I'm fine, thank you,' all the time when really inside I was a mess, an absolute wreck and I didn't have the energy to pretend. But sometimes though, I would smile and say, 'I'm Ok, thanks, how are you?' and then listen to all their goings on for the week. I would walk away and feel pleased, people could talk to me about normal stuff.

People sometimes say the strangest of things: I couldn't believe people would say to me how much better they felt because their life didn't seem so bad when they thought of me. Thanks. Do you think I really needed to hear that!

Over the first couple of years more people began to suggest that I write this book. The seed started to grow within me. At first I remember thinking that I couldn't write, I couldn't write down the reality of what I was going through. Having to relive it all over again and secondly I was useless at English at school; maths was more my thing. But slowly over time I thought that maybe this would help other people, someone out there may be feeling the same as me. They may be alone out there in this world feeling like they are the only person suffering. I wanted to share that this is normal, the pain they are feeling is real and it's Ok to show it, to let it out. To feel suicidal is normal and feeling happy is Ok too, that laughing, a real belly tickler is great. It may be a very long time before you feel it after the pain of loss but one day yes one day you can feel it again and then you start to see that life isn't too bad sometimes. In fact it can be wonderful. The pain is always there, it always will be, but my life is worth living.

So, within a few months of arriving in Cyprus I began to write. I didn't look for work, this book became my life. It hasn't been an easy journey. Writing the details of the court case was probably the toughest chapter for me, at least three loo rolls for the tears and snotty nose, reliving my pain. The final version in this book is probably about a third of what it started as.

I call this all my brain dump. I sit here at my laptop usually in the middle of the night when I would wake with thoughts running through my head. I would just type what I was thinking, downloading my head. I'm glad I learnt to type as I couldn't possibly handwrite as quickly as I can think. The ramblings just pour out of me. But after typing away, sometimes unable to even see the screen for tears, I do feel better. Releasing my pain even further, facing some really tough difficult stuff, but I did it. I have closed so many doors just through writing, so now I look back and am pleased I started. Four years ago I couldn't even write Abigail's name without crying.

My friend Carol who lives here in Cyprus told me about the writers group in Paphos and suggested they might be able to help me. Their meeting was the following day and so I just turned up and introduced myself. I was welcomed with open arms and have never looked back. The throws of life sometimes means that it's not easy to write while other times the words just flow and flow. Sometimes I managed to write thousands at a time, I told you, I'm full of waffle!

The writers group have listened to all my pain and the heartache. They have I feel endured the worst parts of this book. I have often struggled to read my story, feeling the pain once more. I remember one day feeling very proud of myself having read a difficult chapter without too many pauses and tears of my own but when I finished and looked up there wasn't a dry eye in sight. I'm sorry that they have lived through this with me and I am eternally grateful too. Without them this book would without a doubt have never become what it is today. Their advice and support has been invaluable. They have given me encouragement and guidance throughout my journey and boy it has been a tough one.

I have to admit I have never completed any homework that has been set at the group. It's not compulsory anyway but I think they probably would have liked me to have a go. Once I adapted something I had already written to fit, but that's all I've done. I always felt I needed to focus on my book. I found the exercises in the group really difficult to do, after all I never thought of myself as a writer. I just type how I feel, my thoughts and my emotions. A few have suggested I continue to write once the book is finished. I might just surprise them all and go along to the group with a bunch of old homework finally finished, I have lots of catching up to do!

What seems amazing to me now though is that initially I didn't want to write. I didn't want to face the pain I was feeling. I didn't want to have to relive any of it. But the reality is by facing and reliving it I have let out the raw intense emotions and I have been able to let go. Now I am nearing the end of my book. I have booked six nights away in a lovely little village called Bellapais in Northern Cyprus. I'm going to sit and edit my book, I finally feel like a real writer!

'Writing is a good way to release your pain and emotions;

let it all out'

Meditation

While reading a book called 'How to connect with your spirit guide' I asked the question what is next for me, what do I do now? The answer I received quite clearly was to learn to meditate.

A few weeks later while shopping I entered a bookshop and asked at the counter where the books for mediation are. The gentleman guided me to the religious section. Books of all religions and spirituality were there. I was surprised as I hadn't realised that spirituality and religion would be together. I don't know why, I just didn't.

I scanned the books and didn't really know what I was looking for or what I needed. I picked a couple up and flicked through them but none seemed to feel right. I looked around me, the shop was empty so I closed my eyes and asked in my head, 'If this is what I am supposed to be doing please show me what I need to help me.' I opened my eyes and moved my hands across the bookshelf waiting to feel which one was right for me. Weird I know but it worked. I felt the book, picked it up and opened it. I was instantly drawn to the images within the book and liked the style, it just felt right, so I bought it.

I read the book within a week while on holiday in Salou, Spain but I didn't practice the meditations. I felt I needed to read and understand first. When I returned home I wanted to join a class or group to learn this properly. Living in a very remote area it's difficult to find access to anything like this. Still I asked around and searched the internet and one day I fell upon Alternative Vitality in Wick, just round the corner from where I worked, perfect. I called and booked myself onto the next beginner's course which started just a few weeks later. Everything seemed to fall into place.

Donna who owns Alternative Vitality is a very lovely calm lady. I instantly felt welcome in her home where she ran the course. There was a small group of us and I took to meditating straight away. I don't know how but it was like I had found peace within me, my grief and stress all lifted. It was just me and nothing else.

Sometimes it was difficult to clear the clutter in my head and other times it was instantaneous. I could see colours in my mind from the very first time I meditated. I later learned that these are the colours of the chakras within our body. An absolutely beautiful and wonderful experience. I generally see green and purples, very vibrant, moving and swirling it's stunning to watch.

I progressed very quickly and found that I was able to meditate every day. I would get up early and practice even if only for five minutes but generally about half an hour per day. At the end of each session I felt very calm and could proceed with my day practically stress free. If I found myself in difficult situations they seemed easier to deal with and wouldn't cause me any concern. Life became so much easier to deal with on a daily basis. I had found peace inside me.

I progressed to the intermediate and advanced class and found it very easy to meditate for long periods of time. I would receive answers to resolve any problems or concerns I was trying to deal with at the time. I always seemed to be able to find clarity. It's like being the observer of my own life. I can take a step back and sort out the clutter that looked like a tangled mess and slowly straighten everything and work out ways to resolve issues whether they just be ones in my head or physically.

I have since learnt more about the chakras within our bodies, many energy centres within us. There are seven primary ones: the crown, third eye, throat, heart, solar plexus, sacral and root chakra. Each one being a circle of spinning energy with its own colour that works on different parts of our body. When meditating I can see if each chakra is spinning freely and if not I can work with it to clear the clutter and get it spinning effortlessly again. This helps me to feel balanced. It may seem a bit farfetched for some I know but I can assure you it makes a huge difference to how I feel inside and out. I work with my chakras in my yoga practice too as some postures can open them to work more deeply.

I slipped down about four stairs at home early one Friday evening. I couldn't move let alone walk. I found that I could use meditation, focusing on my breath for pain relief while I waited for the ambulance to arrive. I shocked myself and the paramedic when I struggled to lift myself into the chair for them to take me into the ambulance. It wasn't easy or even a quick process but I did it. I didn't want drugs to mask the pain otherwise when arriving at the hospital I wouldn't be able to say where it hurt. I was in distress and suffering intense pain across my back and legs. I was scared, I couldn't walk.

The radiologist had gone home for the evening and wasn't due to return until Monday morning. As I wasn't classed as an emergency I was told if I was still in pain on Monday I would need to go to Inverness hospital. This meant it was more serious than they could deal with. I was prescribed some very strong painkillers and they wanted to keep me in overnight. It was near the time of the anniversary of Abigail's funeral, I couldn't bear to be there and didn't want to stay, the thoughts and emotions running through me too painful.

Monday morning came and I was still flat on my back on Hannah's spare bed in my living room unable to move. Paul called the doctor out. There was no way I could travel to Wick for the x-ray let alone over a hundred miles to Inverness. The doctor arrived, prescribed more painkillers and signed me off work. The medication was making me hallucinate and not really helping with the pain. I decided to alternate them to find out which one was causing the hallucinations. Unfortunately, both of them.

I continued meditating and found I could reduce the intensity of the pain myself so that I could cope without medication. I discussed this with my doctor who was happy for me to continue. My mum went to the natural remedy shop for me in Thurso and came back with a whole host of goodies that I used to help me.

Months later I was still signed off work, I struggled to walk even with crutches. I asked the doctor if I could have an x-ray to determine what was wrong with me. He said there was no point at this stage. They could only assume that I had punched the disks in my spine into my right side and hit my sciatic nerve, causing the pain down my right leg. I was referred for physiotherapy where I also received acupuncture.

It took five months for my recovery until I was able to return to work, but it took well over a year before the pain was reduced to just a dull ache. At times I was terrified that I might never walk properly again. I still have niggles in my back occasionally and I always will, but they are few and far between now. I can go to the gym and exercise generally pain free, I know my limitations.

Now living in Cyprus I have joined a meditation group but have found myself practicing less frequently and it seems to take longer for me to get into a deep meditation. I often find relaxation music, sitting by the sea and yoga helps, but having written this I have realised I need to practice more often. My life seems to be more stressful again at the moment. I need to find that peace within again.

'Finding peace within can be a little bit tricky,

but keep trying, don't give up just yet'

Self Healing

The power of inner peace is incredible. The wisdom within helps us to help ourselves. Easier said than done I know.

I have been on a self destructive journey for the last year. My relationship with Steve has been turbulent to say the least. He would like to describe it as a little "Topsy Turvy." I feel I have been tested to the extreme at times though. I have been an emotional mess and have finally realised that I need to help myself.

It's not easy to have gone through the last year of my life. I separated from Paul and I feel like I have turned Hannah's life upside down. I'm still grieving for Abigail while trying to write this book and then through doing this I have had to relive some of the toughest times over the last five years. I've moved home and started a new relationship with Steve. Any one of these individually is generally challenging, so it's no wonder that my relationship with Steve didn't get off to a good start. I never seem to do things by halves.

But it's hardly surprising that I have been a bit of mess and no-one can help me out of my thoughts and feelings. I need to get myself back on track and the only way forward now is to heal myself. There are many self help books out there and people want to share, support and help but most importantly I have had to come to the bottom rung of the ladder to the deepest darkest place within me to make the decision that I have to do this for myself.

I have always known inside me that only I can do this but along the journey I have always wanted to seek help from others. Now is the time to start the journey alone for healing, to look within, to love and respect myself for who I am. No-one can do this for me, but by doing this I can and will receive far greater respect for myself too.

I have come to terms, if they are even the right words, with my daughters passing, the pain and grief within me will always be there but now is the time for me to stop punishing myself and deal with it. I have searched and searched, received crystal healing, love and support from friends, family and even strangers. I have learnt Reiki and worked with my angel cards to guide me. All this has helped tremendously. I feel now though that I have come to the end of this cycle and now by finding my inner peace I will survive the rest of my life, no longer feeling suicidal.

I have discovered that I am happy being me. I'm happy spending time on my own, doing my own thing and now at last I am ready to face the world as me; Nicola Simpson. The person who I was born to be. An exciting and scary prospect but at last thirty eight years old I am ready to be me. I will always be a grieving Mum and maybe my life purpose is to help others to understand that whatever happens to us in life it teaches us something about ourselves. Whether it is something we like or dislike, we learn from everything that we have to face.

By accepting this, understanding and taking on board the lessons I have learnt, I can only open myself to achieve greater things. Deep I know but so true. I have come to terms with who I am, the mistakes I have made in life, the things I regretted in the past and the wonderful achievements I have made. All have moulded me into be the person that I am today.

It's an old cliché, "You only get one life," but it's true. Get up, get on with it and live it. We should be who we were born to be. I know I wasn't born to be a shrivelled up wreck in the corner, feeling sorry for myself. So every day I get up, get out and get on with it, I face the world. Some days admittedly are much harder than others. I know my life is for living, that's why I'm up and living it. I feel free at last to be me, to live my life. Living with grief is difficult, it will always be there, it will always be part of me. But by accepting grief into my life, by showing my feelings, the real me, people have come to realise who I am. The person within that has been hidden away finally shows through and so I have become aware of who I am and I want to shine.

It's time to learn to love myself for who I am. I am me. I am proud to be me and happy with who I am. My life is special and wonderful; it can only be amazing from here on.

'I'm beginning to love my life again'

So here I am...

Sitting in Cyprus, a lovely country that's hot most of the year. The sun shining on my face, each day brings warmth into my heart. My life has changed completely; I will be a grieving Mum until the end. Hannah is wonderful, a treasure. My beautiful young daughter now fifteen the same age as her older sister. It just doesn't seem fair. It's not right. It's not how life should be. But unfortunately it is our lives and we have to live with it, we have no choice.

My life is going in a completely different direction now. I have no idea really where I'm heading, I take each day as it comes. But I am walking in the joys of life once more.

Cyprus has given me so much more than I imagined. I have had the space I need to unwind and time to grieve. There are so many beautiful beaches where I can relax or snorkel. Even surrounded by people I can, when I choose, escape to my own world alone with my thoughts. I can walk along the road, go shopping or pop out for lunch and nobody knows me here, but most of all I can be myself; a grieving Mum. I have worked through the pain and emotions of living without Abigail, I miss her and I always will. The pain is still here within me, it always will be. The emotions will always return, of course they will, the pain of losing a child is the worst pain of all. But I am living with it.

I get up and look forward to my day. I enjoy painting, meditating, sitting on the beach looking out to sea, going out on the boat to Lara Bay. I even went tuna fishing last year and caught my first fish! A brilliant experience, a memory I will treasure forever.

I love yoga and enjoy every day. I love spending time with Hannah chatting about normal things; her plans for the weekend, boys etc. We miss Abigail and if we could have one wish it would be that she could come home, but reality is, we know she can't.

I have had to explain about Abigail and what happened to so many people here. I will not dismiss her when people ask the nightmare question, 'How many children do you have?'

Abigail is, and always will be part of my family. This has been an extremely difficult journey, the worst of any kind and my journey is far from over. I am looking forward to what the future has in store for me now. None of us know what's round the corner, so it's time to just enjoy the beauty of life.

'Life is for living,

no matter how difficult it may seem sometimes'

A Momentous Day

The feeling is so surreal, did I really just go and meet Scott and his father? That is the question I asked myself as I drove away from their home in Castletown.

Friday 12th August 2011, a landmark date, feels like making history. For months, the last couple of years actually, I have thought about meeting Scott. I knew one day I would. Before travelling back to Caithness from Cyprus last summer I had given it some serious thought as this will be my only opportunity. I hadn't told anyone, I wasn't sure how I felt about it or if I could even do it.

On the Friday afternoon I had met my friends Christine and Dave from John O'Groats along with their grand-daughter for lunch at the Castle of Mey tea rooms. It was lovely to catch up with them. When we left we all drove to Thurso. Christine came in my car so that we could have a good catch up, just the two us. I told her that I had thought about going to see Scott and his dad but I wasn't quite sure how I felt about it or if I was ready. She told me only I could make that decision. No one could tell me what to do. She was right of course. The more I talked the more I realised my only opportunity was today.

Two hours later, after saying goodbye to everyone in Thurso I made my decision to go for it and so I drove to Castletown. As I thought about what I was doing my heart began to pound in my chest, nerves kicking in. Am I doing the right thing? Should I be doing this? I pulled up outside his house. A car parked in the driveway. I guessed someone must be home. My hands shaking, my thoughts racing, but in the blur I got out of the car, locked it and walked up the path to his doorstep and knocked on the door.

His father answered.

'I don't know if I'm brave or stupid,' were the first words that came out of my mouth.

He looked at me, puzzled.

I asked, 'You're Drew?' I knew this as I recognised him from the STV News footage after the court case.

'Yes,' he replied, still looking unsure as to who I was.

'I'm Nicola Simpson . . . Abigail's Mum.'

'Oh . . . come in, come in,' he said, looking shocked.

I stepped into their home, not sure what the hell I was doing turning up on their doorstep, but here I was. I held out my hand offering to shake his. It was very firm. I didn't blame Scott's father and I wanted him to know this. I felt my gesture showed it.

'Scott's upstairs, do you want to see him?' his father asked.

'Oh,' I was surprised, 'yes . . . yes if I could. Would that be Ok?' I thought I would be asking his dad to help me to arrange to meet Scott, I didn't expect to see him right away. But here I was in their house and suddenly everything was happening at once.

'I'll go and ask him and see . . . take a seat,' he said indicating the living room.

I walked into the room and looked at the sofa and two arm chairs. Where should I sit? I thought. I chose the end of the sofa furthest away, next to the fireplace. I saw a photograph of Scott's Mum on the side; she looked so lovely and happy. I sighed to myself and felt their sorrow; having to live without her. Drew came back into the living room and sat on the armchair along from me. Neither of us spoke. Moments later Scott walked into the room and stood in front of the chair, silent and stunned.

'Hi I. . . I . . . I shook your dad's hand. I'm . . . I'm sorry Scott, I can't . . . I can't shake yours right now.' The words tumbled out of me. I had no idea what I was going to say or do at that moment. No anger inside me, just calm and surreal. I was here sitting in their living room.

'I'm . . . I'm . . . I'm so . . . so sorry for what I've done, I'm sorry, sorry. I never meant for this to happen, I'm sorry,' he said as he put his head in his hands and collapsed into the arm chair across from me. Sincerity in his voice, tears in his eyes.

'I know... I know,' was all I could reply. I had heard what I needed to hear.

I explained that I hadn't wanted to go to court but I had gone for Abigail as no-one was there for her. I told him about my letter I had written to the judge asking for a lesser prison sentence and a longer driving ban. Both Scott and his father thanked me.

I told Scott how I hadn't wanted to know what happened after the accident, it was all too raw back then for me to cope with and that I had said I was only prepared to hear about it from Abigail or him.

'I feel that by asking anyone, I am making them relive that night,' I said, 'But if you could . . . could you tell me please?'

He did, breaking down as he got to the part where Abigail was gone. He didn't need to say it, I could hear it in his voice. He couldn't go on; he couldn't speak about it.

I understood. He didn't tell me anything I didn't already know, but I was glad that I had heard it from him. I had needed this for so long, but now I was ready.

I had questions that needed answers, painful but I needed to know. So here I was sat in his home, talking to the person that had caused us all so much pain, who had destroyed all of our lives that night in one fail swoop. A simple mistake without thinking that cost my daughter her life. But still there were things I needed to know, like what was the last song she heard. This had been eating away at me from the moment I was told she died. Now I know and the song fits perfectly, a keepsake in my mind for me. Something I'm not sharing.

We talked about so many things, we even laughed together at times. I knew Scott wasn't an evil horrible bastard and I told him this. I also said that he needs to live his life. I remember him telling me that I shouldn't say such nice things to him. But I meant every word. I remember saying, 'I think we could all do with a dram tonight, I'm off to the Comm later with my friends.'

'Think I'll join you,' his dad laughed.

I turned my head and thought, then said, 'You know what, you would be more than welcome.' I looked at Scott and said, 'Actually it would be nice if you could come and join me for one, but just the one.'

Scott was going to meet his girlfriend later that night and couldn't come, but we agreed we would next time I'm home from Cyprus. That day hasn't come yet, but I'm sure one day it will.

As I left, I stood and shook his father's hand. I stepped towards Scott and held him in my arms. I needed to give him a hug. As we held onto each other he said again that he was sorry. 'I know,' I replied.

I got in my car, sat for a moment stunned, turned the key and pulled away. WOW! I wasn't quite sure how I felt, not sure if amazing could possibly be the right word but it was incredible. It was so surreal, I felt like I'd made history!

I arrived back at Katrina's house where I was staying; I walked in the door and asked for a hug. 'You won't believe what I've just done,' is all I said as I hung on to her sobbing.

'I wish nothing but the best for you now'

Through writing this book and the journey I have taken,

I have come to realise something

I never even thought possible... forgiveness

'I forgive you Scott'

Abigail, I miss you with all my heart

More than words can ever really say

Today, Forever and Always.

All my love

Mum

~ x ~

Lightning Source UK Ltd.
Milton Keynes UK
UKOW03f2242231013

219675UK00015B/805/P